# JOB HUNTING SUCCESS—
# THE KEY QUESTIONS:

What do I really want?
Where do I really want to work?
What company do I want to work for?
What position and salary do I want?
Does my resume express what I have to offer?
Have I acknowledged how first impressions work?
Did I do my homework?
Can my interviewer hire me?
Did I ask for the job?
Have I followed up completely?
Is it still my intention to get the job?
Can I have the job?

The bottom line: You're ready. After reading the invaluable information in *Get a Job in 60 Seconds* and practicing its step-by-step advice you can congratulate yourself on a job well done. Your 60-second count-down to success is complete. Now you are ready to go out and *get that job!*

# GET A JOB IN 60 SECONDS

## Steve Kravette

BANTAM BOOKS
TORONTO · NEW YORK · LONDON · SYDNEY

*This low-priced Bantam Book
contains the complete text of
the original hard-cover edition.*
NOT ONE WORD HAS BEEN OMITTED.

GET A JOB IN 60 SECONDS

*A Bantam Book / published by arrangement with
Para Research, Inc.*

PRINTING HISTORY

*Para Research edition published June 1982*
*Excerpted in* National Employment Weekly *(Wall Street Journal), July 1982.*
*Bantam edition / July 1983*

ISBN 0-553-23568-0

*Published simultaneously in the United States and Canada*

PRINTED IN THE UNITED STATES OF AMERICA

O    0 9 8 7 6 5 4 3 2 1

# Dedication

With love and appreciation,
this book is dedicated to

Jim McLellan,
who willingly and generously
contributed his knowledge,
resources, contacts and energy
as my major external source,

and Jennifer,
who, like always, came through
with the skill and power to
materialize what I want and need.

# Contents

# 0:00

# The Way It Works

There is one thing that's certain in this uncertain world and that's this:

If this book were a job, by the time you read this far you would have gotten it already. Or blown it already.

And if you don't think that's so, you've come to the right place. This book.

It will let you in on the biggest and best-kept secret about job hunting. A secret so big that most employers don't even know what it is, even though they are run by it. A secret so well-kept that even if you've stumbled onto it, you haven't been willing to accept it or believe it.

If, by the way, you do think the opening statement is true and you completely agree with it, you've still come to the right place.

Agreeing means you have an insight or a feeling about the real process of screening and selecting job applicants. If so, this book will sharpen that insight into a finely-honed tool that works by cutting through all the problems, the doubt, the frustration and the anxiety about getting a job. Totally and completely. Whenever you're looking for work.

Either way, you can't lose. Which is how it's supposed to be. In getting jobs. In life. In everything. You see, if you've been losing, it only means that you didn't understand the game. From now on, you will. Especially when it comes to getting a job.

It's worth noting that the same understanding of how the game works applies across the board. You'll get the principle when you see it in other areas.

Here's how the principle works in selecting an apartment, for example. You're looking. As you scan the classified ads, your eye automatically stops on that one. Or that one. That one. And maybe that one. Those are the hot listings for you, the ones you follow up on first. The others don't really count. Without thinking about it, you drop them. And when you call each hot listing, this one or that one no longer looks quite so good to you somehow and you shuffle the others into new positions. Later on, when you go to see the apartments, one instantly is perfect. All the variables match. And if no details turn into insurmountable obstacles, that's the one you pick.

Here's how it works with relationships. You're looking. As you go to parties, bars, seminars or wherever it is that you go to look, your eye automatically stops on that one. Or that one. That one. And maybe that one.

Automatically, you drop all the others. Closer contact and conversation instantly reveal that one or two of your initial choices don't look quite so good anymore and you shuffle the others into new positions. By the time you call them up and go to dinner or a movie or a weekend in the Yucatan, one person is instantly perfect. All the variables match. And if no details turn into insurmountable obstacles, that's the one you pick.

Speaking of dinner, you're looking at the menu. As you run down the possibilities, your eye automatically stops at the shrimp scampi. Or the prime rib. Or the chef's salad. Or maybe the soup 'n sandwich special. One item is always perfect. And if no insurmountable obstacles like price or "out of it" come up, that's the one you pick. It's the job game principle again. Applied to dinners.

Same goes for the movie later on. And the Yucatan after that instead of Miami, Kansas City or Hoboken.

And the same also goes for buying a fall jacket. Selecting a puppy. Checking out the celery or eggplant at the supermarket. You always make your choice on a first impression level. No. No. Yes. No. No. Maybe. That's that. And right after that your mind cuts in and justifies, evaluates, rationalizes and tells you why you made the choice you did. Whether it thinks you were right or not. And whether you should maybe reconsider. That's how it works. That's how it always works. In every area of life.

By now, you can see how the same goes for getting a job. With one obvious and very large exception.

When you want to get a job, it's always someone else's game. Or at least that's the way it seems to you at the time. Because someone else performs the automatic process of making an initial selection from whomever is available. And you are only one of the choices.

By now you know how choices work. The selection is made on an instantaneous first-impression level. Whether your point of entry is a resume, a telephone call or an interview, it's all over after the first five seconds. And it all happened way below any conscious level of thought.

So there's nothing you can do about it. Right?

Wrong.

Like anything else, if you don't know how it works, all you can do is take your chances. And hope.

But if you do know how it works, you can get it to work for you. And in this case, what that means is: getting to work where you want to work. Or getting the job you're after.

In 60 seconds.

The secret of doing that is the essence of simplicity.

All you have to do is keep your prospective employer's unconscious attention focused directly on you (and off everyone else) in a positive way for a total of one minute over the course of your entire interaction together. That means all of your interaction. Resume. Phone calls. Scouting. Interview. Follow-ups. All that.

This book will tell you how. How to make first impressions that have a lasting impact. How to pick up extra points and extra seconds of time in traditional games like resumes and interviews and how to expand into creative nontraditional areas that give you the edge. How to discover and use the power of your own will and your intention to get that job; not any job but that one job you've got to get in order to do what you want to do. How to plan your strategy. How to scout the territory for style, dress codes and good or bad feelings or intuitions about the place. How to follow up. How to get all the way up to the final cut. And beyond it.

How to win, in short, at every stage of the job-hunting game.

Most important of all, this book has been created and organized in a way that will show you how to make the most of the first five seconds of contact. And how to build that one-up connection through a chain reaction of five-second increments all the way up to 60 seconds. At which point you've got the job.

The whole simple secret unfolds: right here. In breathtaking black and white. And it's liberally sprinkled with stories and case histories about how it works, or why it didn't work, in all kinds of industries. From sales, retailing and fast food counters to finance, law and high-tech positions. From Madison Avenue ad agencies, publishers and film studios to top-level Fortune 500 executive suites.

And by the time you finish this book, whatever has been stopping you from getting the kind of job you want will stop stopping you.

You'll know the book worked, by the way, with no questions and no doubts about it. And the way you'll know is: you'll get a job in 60 seconds.

---

## HOW TO GAIN SECONDS

- Notice how you make decisions based on first impressions.
- See how your mind tells you why you made the choice you did, after your first impression.
- Begin to realize that you can control other people's first impressions about you.

# 0:05
# The Best Intentions

OK, now you're willing to win at the job-hunting game or you wouldn't have gotten this far.

To win, you've got to cross the finish line with 60 clear seconds of undivided attention from your prospective employer focused on you.

To cross the finish line, you've got to start at the starting line.

And to start out at the starting line, you've got to warm up, get over to it and be ready to jump in with both feet moving fast when the gun goes off. With no garbage, no banana peels, and no eighteen-wheel, fifty-four-ton trailer trucks in your way.

That's what this chapter is all about.

I want you to stop reading for a minute and get a blank piece of lined paper or take a look at the blank space on pages 9 and 10.

If you're using your own paper, on the top of one side, write a heading that says: The good things about working are. On the top of the other side, write another heading that says: The bad things about working are.

Now turn the paper over to the front and start making a list of as many good things about working as you can think of. Good things like money, new friends, getting ahead, looking successful, coffee breaks, applying your skills. All that stuff. Be sure not to leave anything out. Make a good long list.

No kidding, do it. If you're really serious about getting a job, do it now.

When you're done, turn the paper over and make a list of as many bad things about working as you can think of. That's right, bad things. Like all that time wasted every day, commuting, stupid bosses and other authority issues you may have, whatever else is or was or looks like it could be bad about working.

Tell the truth. Write it down. And make sure you don't leave anything out. Whatever you leave out will knock you out of the running. I guarantee it.

Here's what this is all about.

In many ways, you are probably very much like everyone else in the human race. So you're probably walking around with a really mixed bag of wants, desires, beliefs, thoughts and feelings about getting a job.

Part of you wants to work. Part of you doesn't. Part of you thinks that only drones work from nine to five. Part of you would rather be a brain surgeon or a TV star.

The good things about working are:

_____

_____

_____

_____

_____

_____

_____

_____

_____

_____

_____

_____

_____

_____

_____

_____

_____

_____

_____

_____

The bad things about working are:

_____

_____

_____

_____

_____

_____

_____

_____

_____

_____

_____

_____

_____

_____

_____

_____

_____

_____

_____

Part of you wants to be rich and believes you have to work to do it. Part of you hates how hard your dad had to work to make ends meet. All that.

What is important is for you to begin to become aware of how you feel about working.

You've got to know what all your particular wants, desires, beliefs, thoughts and feelings about getting a job are, so that you can live with them and take them along with you consciously when you go to get a job.

You see, you'll take them with you anyway. You always do. But if you don't write them down, look at them, acknowledge that you have them, get your patterns of behavior clarified, and be honest with yourself about it all, you'll take them with you unconsciously. And they'll keep getting in your way.

I spoke with fifty-six employers in just about every field. I asked each of them what was wrong and what was right about the applicants they had been getting. Better than 90 percent of them told me that most of the people who come in for jobs act like they're just going through the motions and don't really give the impression of caring about working.

My opinion is that many of us actually don't care about working one way or the other. And if every one of our personal wants and needs dropped out of the sky every morning and landed in a neat pile at the foot of our beds, all the commuter trains and buses and expressways would begin to look awfully empty during rush hours.

My opinion is also that the people who get job offers are the ones who fully acknowledge to themselves how much and in exactly what ways they really don't want to work. And who also fully acknowledge to themselves how much they intend to create and to have the benefits that a job will bring.

So if you're someone, for example, who is naturally a little lazy or perhaps even a lot lazy, just put that on your "Bad Things" list and notice it. That's all. Don't do anything about it. Just notice it and stop hiding it. Also notice that you have a lot of other considerations in addition to being lazy. Like wanting to eat every day, or being rich and famous or acclaimed. And that no single consideration is bigger or better or worse or more or less meaningful than any other.

Notice that all your considerations are just there. Just like your nose, your jacket, your ballpoint pen, your capped tooth and the spot on the floor.

The fact is, some of the best workers in the universe are people who take their considerations about laziness very seriously. And indulge them regularly. Off the job.

On the job, they choose to indulge their other considerations about working instead.

That's what the lists are for. So you can notice whether or not there's anything you need to become aware of. On the way to the starting line.

The point is this. Wanting a job isn't enough. Needing a job isn't enough. Wishing and hoping for a job isn't enough. Positive thinking about a job isn't enough. And dragging yourself out in the world with all your withheld considerations and thoughts about working and going through the motions is definitely not enough.

Before you make your first approach, and your first approach is the point at which employers make their first impression, you've got to get really clear about what your intention about getting a job is. And then you've got to bring your body, your emotions, your thoughts, your pictures, your previous successes and rejections and all the rest of you into a state of alignment on your intention.

Intention happens at a level outside of your ordinary awareness. It is used to determine the course and outcome of events in your life. When you are in touch with that particular level of awareness, each new event becomes an opportunity for new experiences instead of surprises, problems, or someone dumping on you. When you realize that you use your power of intention to actually create the events that you experience, you get to choose between being satisfied and nurtured by what happened or being victimized, angered or depressed by it.

Either way, you always get exactly what you intended. Always. And in all ways.

Here is how to discover the way intention works. And how to use it concretely and specifically.

Before you begin the process of looking for a job, make up a game. Give the game a name. Call it: "Getting A Job." And then bring all of your resources and talents into the game in a way that ensures winning.

It's easier done than said.

Just follow these steps.

**Set up the game.** The game is "Getting A Job." Whose game is it? Yours? That's right. Never forget that it is your game. And that you get to say who wins and who loses. And how.

**Set up the rules.** The game will last fifteen or thirty or sixty days or whatever you say. The game ends when you have a new job. To be a big winner, the job must be (fill in a job description) and the job must pay at least (fill in a bottom-line salary). For the period of the game, you agree to play full tilt. No holding back. No saving some for next time Those are the rules. Now, whose rules are they? Are you sure? From now on, please make it a point to always remember that in this game the rules are your rules.

**Check out the rules.** Are you being too reasonable? Did you make the game too easy and boring? Or did you make the game too hard and demanding? The idea is not to be reasonable. If you pay attention to statistics, and I suggest that you don't, you'll notice that getting a job is not reasonable these days. Too many people, not enough opportunities, cutbacks, inflation, you name it. So don't try to play a reasonable game in an unreasonable world. On the other hand, don't limit yourself, or make it too hard on yourself. Getting a job as a salesperson who handles only green and brown speckled beach rocks less than one and one-half inches in diameter in the western Milwaukee area will make the game more difficult than it needs to be. Given enough time and enough intention, you can get even that job. But why make yourself crazy? And why wait? Especially when 60 seconds is all you're going to need.

Just for the record, a difficult game is no better than an easy game. It's also no worse. As long as you're making up the game at all, make the game challenging and fun. It's no fun to play games with babies who always lose or with computers that always win.

**Check out yourself.** Are you really willing to own the game you made up and take full responsibility for its creation? Are you really willing to follow the rules, your rules? Are you really up to playing full out within the time frame you established? And are you willing to bring 100 percent of you into the game? Which means including all your fears about rejection, all your past screw-ups, all your anger about interviewers or evaluators, all your hopes, all your ideas about why not working is better than working. Be sure you can include all of it, everything you hold and carry with you. And be sure you have identified as much of that as you can, so you know precisely what you are including.

**Declare yourself.** Tell everyone you know (except your co-workers and supervisor if that's not appropriate) that you are going to get a job by the date you chose and tell them all exactly what kind of job it will be. Go into detail. Once you get in touch with your intention by creating the game and making it a reality by committing yourself to it and declaring it to be true, there's no turning back. You set in motion the machinery that will enable you to materialize whatever it takes to win your game. In the beginning, there is always the word. In the beginning of getting a job there is your word. You give your word about what you are going to do. And then you keep your word. By going out and doing what you said you would do. After that, you get to take satisfaction in the results.

When you create your own game you can make the job you'll get fit your needs. If you examined the best and worst things about working and discovered you are truly lazy, you can set up a game that gets you a job you work at for two hours a day. Or for two days a week.

If you examined the best and worst things about working and discovered that you love the kind of a job at which you work twelve hours a day, set up a game that will get you that job.

It's your game. Design it to get the job you want. NOT the job someone else says you need.

Using your power of intention is the one and only way you have to be in complete charge and take absolute responsibility for getting a job, without being tossed and buffeted by fate, conditions, circumstances and other people.

In the first chapter when I told you how choices are made, I said it always seems like someone else's choice when you're getting a job. It only seems that way because you never consciously made it your game before.

So intention is how to take over and own the whole experience, how to make it your own game. And what you need to remember is that if you don't become the cause of your experience and take full responsibility for creating every bit of it every moment of every moment, you will be stuck with the alternative. Which is to be at the effect or the result of whatever happens to you next. With reaction as your only recourse instead of creation as your only choice. You'll know when you're at effect because it always looks like they are doing it *to* you. And you always feel done in and swept under by the events of your life.

Get in touch with your intention right now. And use it and this chapter as the foundation and the fuel that will get you to the starting line of getting a job.

---

## HOW TO GAIN SECONDS

- Acknowledge each and every one of your good and bad points.
- Get clear about your intention.
- Set up your own job game.

# 0:10

## First Impressions

Look up for a moment. And notice the first person who comes along who you don't know. If you're at home, step outside and see who walks by.

No kidding. You really need to take the time to do this to experience the point.

And the point is this.

If you tune in to what's going on, you'll become aware that you didn't see the person you saw.

You saw your internal pictures of the person you saw, superimposed over the person as he or she really was. You saw your thoughts and evaluations and judgments about what the person must really be like. You may even have seen your fears and prejudices instead of seeing the person.

For instance, you could have seen a man all dressed up in loud clothing and a wide-brimmed leather hat and a lot of gold jewelry. And you could have seen him step into the back seat of a large white Cadillac in which two flashy-looking women were sitting.

Probably you also saw a story about what you thought he was and what you thought he did for a living. Probably you didn't give reality a chance to reveal the true story to you, the way reality always does whenever you give it even half a chance.

Instead, you jumped to conclusions. And you let your first impressions take over.

Guess what? I know the man who got into that Cadillac. And he isn't what you thought he was. He happens to be a dentist.

The personnel manager of one of the country's biggest financial corporations told me, "I'd never want my department to know I said this, but I am always looking at my own prejudices whenever an applicant comes into my office for the first time.

"I want to hire someone who looks and thinks like I do. Someone who will fit into this corporation like the other people here.

"So the first things I see are the differences. All the reasons why not. And I've made my mind up before I ask the first question.

"Sometimes the rest of the interview will change my mind. But it's an uphill struggle most of the way. And I still have those first intangible thoughts about why this person doesn't fit in flashing on and off on some subliminal level.

"It also works the other way. If I get someone in here who's a perfect fit, I know that too. Long before the first question. Hardly anything that gets said or done will be strong enough to change my first impressions about basic rightness."

Do you get it? You'd better. More than fifty people responsible for hiring other people agree. Some more, some less.

They and all their counterparts do the same thing you do when you see someone for the first time. Except they do it to you.

You come up against their first-impression mechanism three times whenever you play your Getting A Job Game. When they receive your resume or letter. When you or they call to arrange an interview. And most of all, when you walk into their office.

You'll get all the details about how to buy your 60 seconds of time by handling each area later in this book. For now, just stick with the first-impression level. And take a look at what can go wrong or go right.

The president of a national recruiting and placement firm says, "At my company it takes 1,200 resume contacts to make one hire. That means we send out 1,200 of our clients' resumes to one company or one resume to 1,200 companies. Those are not good odds.

"On the resume level, you're only a number, a statistic.

"On a personal level, on the other hand, one in nine gets hired. So you've got an 11 percent chance and five interviews will usually get you a job.

"The trick is to get out of the resume trap."

In other words, being just one resume in a large pile is not the way to get a job in 60 seconds. Or 60 years.

Back in the days when I was creative director at an ad agency, I was the person who hired all the other writers. I remember how I could take all the resumes I received every month, throw them across my office, and know who I'd want to talk to from seeing the resumes upside-down in a pile twelve feet away.

It always has to do with style, presentation, neatness and the feel of the paper and the envelope as much as the content.

On the first-impression playing field, more often than not, your resume is your least reliable asset. In 0:25, you'll find some useful and specific suggestions on how to improve the odds by making your resume work harder.

If you have to be in touch with your interviewer before your appointment, or if a call is necessary to set up your appointment, keep it short.

Complete your call before a first impression is formed. And you'll be in the best possible shape. It's not easy for someone to form pictures of you over a fast businesslike telephone talk unless your vocal presentation is unusually good or unusually poor.

When you sound very impressive or glamorous or sophisticated, you'll be expected to look the part in person. Or else.

When you sound particularly nasal or tiny-voiced or just plain odd, it will work against you. Even further back in the old days when I stuttered badly on the telephone, potential employers always knew who I was when I came to see them. They'd say, "Oh, you're the one who stutters. Well, you just relax during this interview. Tell me, do you have that problem all the time?"

It's not exactly the best setup for a fair and unbiased evaluation.

So calls that are short and to-the-point are the calls that win. Especially when you end on a cheery and positive note about "looking forward to getting together with you."

But even on the telephone, expect surprises. Personnel people do. One engineering firm, known for hiring no more minority employees than the law requires, offered a job to a man named Peter Clarke III on the strength of his resume, his degrees, and his strikingly cultured telephone voice. Peter, an Indian from India, showed up for work in a turban.

By far, first impression opportunities are created or demolished during the first five seconds of the first interview.

Think back to that person you saw at the start of this chapter when you looked up and noticed someone. Five seconds is always all it takes.

If that's not clear to you yet, put down the book. Get up. And notice the first person you see right now. Do it again and see how the process works.

They'll look at you and what they'll see is this. Too fat. Too thin. Too macho. Too feminine. Too blonde. Too black. Too short. Too sexy. Too wide a tie. Too long a skirt. Dirty fingernails. I don't like redheads. Intellectual. Wimp. Too powerful. Too quiet. Arrogant. Jerk. Nice legs.

All this in five seconds. And more.

You'll be measured, drawn and quartered, and dissected by totally nonobjective criteria.

In fact, the person you see may be one of the corporate officers, personnel managers or interviewers who told me:

"I'm biased against backyard and hometown people. Someone who walked over here from down the street can't be very special."

"I never hire the first person I interview. God could walk in here first and I'd turn him down. Someone better always shows up later in the day."

"Having a job already is important. If they don't have one, they're no good."

"The right person can walk in here and I'll see to it that a job gets created for him."

"I used to be very shy, so I empathize with shy people and tend not to like extroverts or a person who comes on too strong."

"I relate best to people who ground it out and busted their backs working their way through college, just like I did. More fortunate applicants are definitely starting off at a disadvantage around me."

"The woman from the employment agency turned me down again when I asked her out to dinner last week. You think I'll hire anyone *they* send me?"

"It's not easy finding anyone these days. That's why they hired me, a consultant, to recruit people. When I find them all, I lose *my* job. Look, times are tough. I may never find them. You know what I mean?"

Just to make things a little worse, when you have a two-stage interview (in which the personnel person screens you and then takes you to meet your potential supervisor) the first impression you made during the first interview goes along with you. On a little note attached to your application and resume.

The notes read like this:

"Intelligent guy, good background, sort of articulate. Someone should tell him his fly is open."

"Nice gal. Attractive. Strong. Aggressive. But looks like a real cold cookie."

I saw those notes. They're real. What do you suppose those two people got? They certainly didn't get hired.

The national sales manager for a well-known sporting goods brand offers this advice. "Chances are, the first thing I see when I look at an applicant is the first thing all the retailers he'll call on will also see, after he gets a job with me.

"If my impression is favorable, warm, friendly, theirs will be too. And getting along with them is what counts around here. I used to be one of them. so I know.

"Win me over fast and you'll get any job I've got in 60 seconds. Maybe less."

You can see what you're up against on a first-impression level. Later on, you'll see what to do about it.

But before you fade into quiet despair about first impressions, here comes the good news.

First impressions are a two-way street.

Your first impressions of them are just as appropriate or inappropriate as their first impressions of you.

Expect to notice that you're having yours at two completely different stages of your Job Game. When you scan the ads or listings. And when you show up at your side of the interview desk.

Before you look over the ads in newspapers, magazines or recruitment agency listings, be sure you have looked over the rules of your Getting A Job Game. You know, the game you created in 0:05.

Know what your goals and wants are. In position. In salary. In opportunity to advance and learn new skills. And measure each ad you read against your current objectives.

Even the shortest, most concise want ads will offer clues and indicators about whether they are appropriate choices or not.

When your game rules are clear and your goals are solid, you can trust your intuition and your first impressions.

Your internal computer will tell you which ads you have to answer, which ads you just might answer, and which ads you can forget about.

Now, a word about those ads you absolutely have to answer.

Don't.

Don't answer them. You're just not ready to do anything about those ads yet. Later, after you've read the next three chapters and done the work in them, you'll be ready. And when that happens and you answer your favorite ad, here's a little secret way to produce results against overwhelming odds.

Cut out the one ad that represents the job you want most, the one you'd do anything to get. And carry it with you in your wallet every day and put it under your pillow every night. Keep in solid physical contact with it all the time until you get your job.

And you will get your job.

This solid representation of what you want works for you. It's a constant reminder of your intention. It won't make sense. But it will make a connection possible that can materialize the job for you.

Just remember not to do that or anything else until you've completed the next three chapters.

Your second set of first impressions will form when you go for your interview. Notice your nervousness, fear, doubt and uncertainty. And let them be the way they are. Never, never lie to yourself about how you are feeling.

Beneath that level, begin to notice what you think about the place you've gone for your interview. Become aware of how you feel about it and how you react to the people and the decor and the atmosphere there.

These are your first impressions and your first indicators about whether or not the job is right for you.

Maintain this level of awareness when you meet your interviewer. Be sure to notice your thoughts, pictures and feelings. Whom does he remind you of? What do you like or dislike about him?

Your first impressions count.

An interviewer who reminds you of Uncle Albert who always brought you Tootsie Rolls will have a different effect on you initially than one who reminds you of mean old Miss Craignaut, the second grade teacher who always picked on you.

Notice your impressions. And remember: the person you're looking at is neither Uncle Albert nor Miss Craignaut. It's somebody else altogether. Somebody who will probably give you the job you want if you don't get confused about that one fact.

Once you get this far in becoming aware of your mental processes, you can be sure of four things. You will be more relaxed. You will be more yourself. You will be more aware of whether this is really the job for you. And, for sure, you will be five seconds closer to getting the job you want.

---

## HOW TO GAIN SECONDS

- Remember that first impressions become hard-core reality. Unless you control how they work.
- First impressions matter most when the employer receives your letter or resume, when you call to arrange an interview and when you walk into the office.
- Create and play your own Job Game.

# 0:15
## Staying Alive

OK, it's time to take another look inside yourself. So use page 29 or get another blank piece of paper. And on one side at the top, write a heading that says: The best thing about me is.

Then fill out the rest of the section with every best thing about yourself that you can bring to mind.

Cover what's special about you. What's unique. What the high point in your life is and what the high point in your work has been so far. What is definitely great about you and your abilities.

The best thing about you might be: Your looks. Your Phi Beta Kappa key. Your new car. Your 1979 sales award. Your husband. Your skill as a lover. Your last raise. Your ability to visualize. Your voice. Your bowling score. Any of those things. Or all of them.

Don't worry if some of the best things have nothing to do with your work. Just write down every best thing you can conjure up. And be sure to cover everything before you stop.

By now, you know these little exercises work. So do this one.

Then, before you think about it too much, use page 29 or turn your paper over and write this heading: What I don't want them to find out about me is.

Fill in the section listing all the things about yourself that you hide. Things that would embarrass and mortify you if anybody knew. Things that have a way of running your life by surfacing all the time unexpectedly because you have so much energy devoted to hiding them.

Things like: Your fear of elevators or snakes or intimacy. Your nosepicking. Your jailbird father. The time you stole something from the Five and Ten or from your last employer. Anxiety. Drug addiction or alcoholism. The time you cheated on your spouse. The time you did that awful thing, whatever it was. How much you really need this job. Once again, list any of these things or your own equivalent things. List everything you hide. All of it.

This is your one big chance to acknowledge what you hide. And what you overemphasize in some way to make up for what you're hiding.

It's important for you to know both. And guess who is the only one who can tell you.

So tell yourself before you go any further. On that piece of paper. In writing.

In case you haven't guessed why you just did that, I'll tell you why.

The best thing about me is:

_____

_____

_____

_____

_____

_____

_____

_____

_____

What I don't want them to find out about me is:

_____

_____

_____

_____

_____

_____

_____

_____

_____

What makes a first impression positive or negative depends 100 percent and absolutely on how much of yourself you are willing to reveal to someone else. Openly and honestly. Yourself. Just the way you are. With nothing added and nothing left out.

That doesn't mean offering to have a true confessions session or presenting a boring rundown of your attributes. It means, whenever you reveal yourself to the world, simply be fully aware of exactly who you are and how much you are choosing to put out or to hide.

Just for the record, I bet you think all the things on the best side of the page are really good. And all the things on the hiding side are really bad.

Guess again.

There is no difference. None at all. In fact, often it works just the opposite of the way you think it works.

For instance, I personally would find it a lot more interesting to hear about the time you wanted to make love with your cat than to hear about your fourth-grade penmanship award. But that's not the point.

The point is that the part of you that shows is the sum total of all your experience. None of it is really good in an absolute sense. And none of it is really bad. All of it contributed to bringing you to the point you are at right now.

All of it is woven into the content of your life.

And all of it makes you who you are.

Now, you've got to get this next part if you want to go any further.

What someone else says doesn't make you who you are. And what someone else thinks or feels or surmises doesn't make you who you are either. Only you have the power to make you who you are.

There is a widespread myth about needing to evaluate everything, including you. And judge it. And compare it to other things and other people. That's all it is. A myth. It doesn't mean anything at all.

But even though you know it's a myth and doesn't mean anything at all, you still react differently to "best things" and "hiding things" out of fear of being judged and evaluated and compared. Somebody once told you all that stuff was important and you believed them.

Well that somebody lied, whoever they were.

All judging and evaluating and comparing is only what someone says it is. And just because someone says it doesn't make it so.

Who makes it so for you? You do.

Terrific.

So those things you've been hiding and those things you've been shoving down everybody's throats as great moments in your history have cost you something.

What they've cost you is your aliveness. Your sense of yourself. Yourself as the beautiful and wonderful creature you really are.

Yes, you. The one with all those rotten things on your list of things you don't want them to find out about.

Until now, instead of who you are, you've been someone who thought they needed to justify and defend someone's unacceptable judgments and positions about who you really are and what you are worth.

Look at it this way.

Are you really only an item on your list like stealing a box of magic markers or a typewriter? Or swearing at someone you love the last time you got angry? Or copulating with the cat? Could it be that you're that small?

Or are you a lot bigger than that?

Are you really only an item like being a great dresser? Or being first in productivity in your department?

Or are you a lot bigger than that, too?

Chances are, you are one hell of a lot bigger than you think. And that bigness, when expressed, takes the form of aliveness, enthusiasm and twinkle-eyedness.

That's what works when you're looking for a job. That's what keeps the clock running toward the 60-second "Got It" mark.

The vice president of a graphic arts company had an opening for a high-level sales position. "Sixty-five people made it to the final cut. And less than four of them even sounded alive, much less looked it, when they showed up.

"With all these so-called best people coming across as bored or dead, I was about to give the job to a woman who walked in with no previous sales experience at all. She was so bright and alert and enthusiastic that I knew she'd learn fast and be great in the field.

"She would have gotten the job. But at the last minute someone else called who had all those things plus an impressive seven-year track record on-the-road.

"That woman's going to be the next person I hire here though. I told her so. First chance I get, I'll steal her away from whoever she ends up with now.

"Whenever I see a quality of aliveness and enthusiasm like that, I want to have it around here. And I know that instantly."

A personnel manager at a large department store says, "Except for crisis situations like the holidays when almost anything or anyone goes, I always know who's going to get hired here.

"The key is enthusiasm. A sparkle in the eyes. Someone who can get a positive response from tired, cranky, angry customers will always get one from me."

Over and over again, from a McDonald's manager to the personnel manager of one of America's largest corporations, one of the keywords today is "aliveness."

And aliveness is what you have when you are simply you. With nothing added and nothing left out.

Maybe one of the things you've been trying to hide, for instance, is a self-evaluation that you're not very good-looking. So you comb your hair all over your face and dress in a manner that draws attention away from you and onto something that you are wearing.

People know. They know exactly what you don't want them to know. Worse than that, you're always the last one to find out that they know.

So if you're out to get a job and you think your looks may get in your way, don't stiffen up or cover up or fake it. Let your considerations about your looks contribute to your presentation.

You might say something like, "I've got to tell you this. I may not be the best-looking person in the world. Some people even think I'm sort of ugly. But, boy, am I ever willing to work to do a great job here. You can count on me for that."

Do you know what honesty like that gets you?

It gets you hired.

Because whenever you release the energy you use to hold on to something that you hide, that energy rushes through your body and lights you up. It makes you look and feel alive. In a way that makes you just about irresistible.

That's how to become alive.

To stay alive, keep tuning into yourself when you're playing your Get A Job Game.

Keep asking:

Am I hiding?

What am I hiding?

How can I turn that around and share it in a way that will enliven me?

Am I staying too long on something that I want them to think is good about me?

What don't I want them to know that I am using my "good me" story to mask?

Keep on noticing things like that and you know what? You'll definitely be another five seconds closer to getting a job in 60 seconds.

And you'll be staying alive too, so that you can really enjoy it.

---

## HOW TO GAIN SECONDS

- Identify what you like about yourself and what you want to hide.

- Get the idea that your conceptions about your good things and bad things makes no difference. Everything you do is just you.

- Be enthusiastic. Ninety percent of potential employers say people coming in and asking for jobs act as if they don't care.

# 0:20
# Your Problems Are All Behind You

It's funny how backgrounds always keep butting into the foregrounds of your present experience in life. And how, frequently, what you did seems more significant to other people than who you are and what you are doing now.

But since that's the way it comes up in your Job Game, now is the time to look into all the ways your background and qualifications can add precious seconds to the 60 you need to get the job.

Yes, *your* background. Flawed and scarred as it may be.

The head of a large publishing house recommends, "Have a job now; come from a thousand miles away or more; make me steal you from your present employer (naturally a big name company); show me a Master's degree, a happy marriage, two or three kids, a well-typed resume; be on the way up with no more than four successful career jumps; also be good-looking, well-dressed and from a socio-economic-religious background that fits the company image here. Do that and I'll hire you in a minute."

"A lot of my jobs fit certain women's temperaments best. Like an older, newly single woman," confided a retail chain's vice president. "They need the job more. And they won't run off and get married on me."

"Harvard and Yale Law School graduates only," says the senior partner of a prominent law firm. "Others aren't worth the time. Let the schools weed them out."

That's how it is sometimes. But don't let it worry you. This chapter will even the odds for everyone who doesn't fit these particular criteria for an ideal past.

You may notice that in job categories where there is more than the usual high degree of competition, you'll also find more than the usual amount of arrogance on the part of many employers. That just has to be OK the way it is. Especially if that *is* the way it is. And, if that's so for you, ask yourself what you have to do with creating that kind of arrogance in your Job Game and in your life.

As far as your own background is concerned, everything you are about to read is true.

"You cut right through the competition when you've chosen to make a couple of major career jumps with the right companies." From a corporate VP.

"Never take a job that's not on target for you. One fellow I interviewed took six months off to help a friend start a business in a completely unrelated field. He could do that again sometime, just on a whim. But he won't do it to me." From a retailer's personnel manager.

"Stick with name organizations. A good name can impress me enough to make up for a lack of solid credentials. It proves someone is used to discipline, pressure, on-timeness. I've got a woman here in my accounting department whose background reads 'Two years, maintenance staff, IBM. Two and a half years, typist, General Electric. One year, security staff, Xerox.' She happens to be a natural whiz with software accounting programs though. And besides, I liked her courage." From a savings bank vice president.

On the other hand, in many ways everything you have just read is not true.

You see, one of the nice things about creating your own Job Game, as you did in 0:05, is that you get to create with whom you'll be playing it, what they'll think about you, and what they'll want from your background.

What I want you to know about backgrounds is this. You have to carefully pick and choose the parts that are relevant. And you have to forget about the rest of it.

Logical, right?

You just won't have time to cover everything from your birth to this moment. No one expects you to either. So choose what you use. And make the most of it.

It's not hard to choose.

Start with your list of "The best thing about me is" and pull out all the best things that relate to your present focus on getting a job.

Add whatever you can think of that would knock the socks off someone with job requirements as narrow as some of the ones you just read about.

You already have everything you need to get a job anywhere you want. All you have to do now is start to use it properly and effectively.

A few for-instances.

If you're fresh out of school with a liberal arts degree and no experience, tell how that qualifies you. In terms of youth, energy, trainability, grades, summer job, success stories and hobbies that relate to your field of interest. (For instance, model building supports your intention to become an industrial designer, but ballet dancing doesn't.) You know that you are much more interesting than anybody else. You've always known that, deep inside. So pull out all the pieces from your past that support that being true.

If you're moving into a bigger league from a series of jobs with no-name employers, stress what you did and how that made a positive contribution to each of them. Maybe you were responsible for a procedural change or a morale improvement that increased efficiency by 15 percent. Whatever you did, now is the time to show off about it. And tasteful showing off will tip the scales and the clock your way. Even if you never came within five hundred miles of New York Life or Exxon.

If you have something you want to hide, think about that now. Take out your list and see what you're hiding that relates to work.

Perhaps it seems like a big problem. Like getting fired. But maybe it's not so bad.

Look at it this way.

First of all, it may not come up. And if it doesn't, don't volunteer. Never volunteer anything negative.

Plan ahead though. And know exactly what you'll say if it does emerge. So you won't get caught sitting there with your head buried under your elbow or in some more picturesque part of your anatomy, not getting that job.

Getting fired or anything "bad" like that always has more than one side. Sometimes there are even more than two sides. It all has to do with how you present the material.

When you're confronted with it or there's simply no way to hold it back, consider telling the truth. Acknowledge getting fired. Then tell how there was this general cutback right around the time you were having a personality conflict with your supervisor.

Tell whatever really happened. Don't fake the facts. Just choose the facts that can help you. Then very briefly state what you learned from the experience and how that knowedge will benefit your next employer's company.

Telling the truth works.

Lying about your background usually doesn't. But not for the reasons you think, and certainly not for the reasons they told you in Sunday School.

Lying creates an atmosphere of furtiveness, of withholding, of hiding the lie, and then lying even more to hide the lie about the lie, and lying still more to hide the lie about the lie about the lie.

You become more concerned about what you are trying to hide than you are about getting the job. And the person interviewing you eventually catches on.

Like the time the personnel director of a large corporation checked a key employee's file, out of friendly curiosity, during a college recruitment trip to the man's Alma Mater. "Not only didn't the guy have a degree, he didn't even attend that university. When I got back and asked him about it, he told me he had worked for the C.I.A. and that they had 'disappeared' all his records. Can you imagine that?"

Another famous lie came to light in 1980. A reporter for the *Washington Post* won the Pulitzer Prize for a story she made up. She had also made up the credentials that got her the job at the *Post* in the first place. She lied about her college degree, her master's degree and her experience abroad. When the national publicity about her Pulitzer appeared, her background became big news. Institutions that would have loved to have claimed her as a graduate honestly couldn't. They revealed the lies and a very imaginative reporter lost her job, lost her Pulitzer and probably lost her credibility in her profession forever. In fact, when she tried to get a job at another newspaper, the reporters there strongly protested and blocked her being hired.

When you lie, you progressively shut down pieces of yourself. Until you're completely shut down.

Remember how important aliveness is?

Because lying shuts you down, it kills off aliveness. So it will not assist you in getting your job in 60 seconds.

Knowing that much about lying, you'll want to take a long hard look at whether or not you really want any job that you would have to lie to get. It may just not be worth the price.

Unfortunately or not, the truth is that a lot of success stories about getting jobs have been based on lies. On a superficial level, it's easy to get away with lying. A lot easier than anyone thinks.

The director of a national recruitment firm says, "There is no practical way to verify employement records or college transcripts. When we check, three out of four inquiries never get answered. So we can't verify whether a grade average is 1.8 or 4.0. We also can't check jobs claimed to have been held at defunct or imaginary firms. And we can't get verification about bad work experiences. The law won't allow that last one.

"To further complicate things, in some fields like nuclear energy, standards change. People now at work couldn't get their same jobs again because more advanced degrees are now required.

"You'd be surprised how little actual checking ever gets done. And how sloppy the results of each inquiry actually turn out. People can get away with almost anything if they brazen it out!"

So can you, and I recommend that you don't. You can't afford it. The price is your aliveness. And aliveness is the only thing you've really got going for you.

The last issue about background is this: Be realistic.

Deal exclusively with your next employer's bottom line requirements. "Brain surgeons never get picked to be engineers around here," notes a corporate vice president with a grin. "And they won't find too much work for $5 an hour either."

Look at what you like to do. And look at what you do well. Then choose what you want to do.

After that, just get up a Job Game that lets you do exactly that.

All right. Now that you've taken a look at your background and what's involved, it's time to take a look at their background.

Their background is a lot more important that yours. Here's why: when they know all about you, you may or may not get the job. But when you know all about them and other applicants don't, you will definitely get the job.

Knowing about their background is worth at least five seconds. And, more important, it's the ultimate equalizer for spots, holes, or pimples on your own background.

"If you're still a student, take on the investigation of your first employer as if it was the one term paper your grades depended upon. If you've had a job, learn as much about your prospective employer as you know about your past one." Good advice from a personnel interviewer at a machine tool corporation.

Be sure you know exactly what your company-to-be makes and what services it offers. Also know what's new. Both at the company and in the industry.

To start, the place to go for general data is your library. Later on, I'll show you some supersleuth techniques for finding out almost anything on your own.

By the way, you'll never be able to check out 1,200 companies so don't even try. This book is not about playing large numbers to increase the odds. It's about getting exactly the job you want at one of a few selected companies. So do just that.

The library and a little digging will give you the general background stories you need to know before you take any active steps or answer any ads.

For the record, I'll give you that again. *Don't do anything until you've checked out the company and its management. Don't even consider it.*

Your librarian can show you where to begin. Then you can look up the standard sources yourself. Include these:

>    Chamber of Commerce publications.
>
>    Dun & Bradstreet's Million Dollar Directory.
>
>    Encyclopedia of Business Information.
>
>    Fitch Corporation manuals.
>
>    Fortune's latest 500 issue.
>
>    MacRae's Blue Book.
>
>    Moody's Industrial Manual.
>
>    National trade journals, annuals and directories.

Plan Purchasing Directory.

Professional association publications.

Redbook of Regional Corporations.

Standard & Poor's Corporation Records, Industrial Index and Listed Stock Reports.

Statistical Abstract of the U.S. Department of Commerce.

Thomas' Register of Manufacturers.

Walker's Manual of Far Western Corporations and Securities.

Insights about the management of leading corporations, including the name of the person you want to contact and be interviewed by, are plentiful in *Who's Who*.

Be sure to notice what characteristics senior management has in common. By finding out where management is coming from and finding out as much as you can about their point of view, you'll know what any corporation is all about. You'll also be ahead of everyone else when you look for common ground in your interview.

Read recruitment brochures, any company publications you can get your hands on, trade ads and industry newsletters.

Company newspapers give you useful insider's information about what's going on and who's making decisions about what, including hiring you.

Use library reference materials to check out the background of any company you want to apply to before you apply. That means, check out the company behind any ad you clip before you answer it.

If you liked the sound of a blind ad (one with no name and only a box number), see whether you can pick out enough clues from the content of the ad to pinpoint the company that ran it.

For instance, if you're reading a blind box ad for a large photographic company in the Northeast, don't write to the box number, write to Polaroid. Use your imagination to break through the blind spot. Go for positive identification. If you can't do that, make an educated guess. Send your resume. Then go and check them out.

If you can't come up with a name, forget it. Save the ad for reference about wording and the kind of qualifications that someone you'd like to work for is seeking. And let it be. For now, I can promise you that jobs in blind ads are never ever jobs that you can get in 60 seconds, unless you crack the code and identify the company. Take my word for it. You'll see why in the next chapter.

These are some ads you should avoid.

> WANTED: One person to do everything. Apply Box ,C-1, New York Globe.

Unless you can guess the company, avoid blind box ads.

> We have thousands of positions open. One of them is perfect for you. We'll place you where you belong. Write Box 007, Los Angeles Daily.

Probably a personnel agency looking for people. Avoid it unless becoming involved with an agency is part of your Job Game.

> We need a shirt sleeve executive.
> Call 222-9999.

Beware of phone numbers. If you do call, just schedule an interview. Don't let them interview you over the phone.

> NEEDED: Three people to do the worst job in the world. It's low pay, long hours, but you'll be investing in your tomorrow.

Avoid ads that sound negative. You can literally have it all. A good tomorrow and an even better today.

By the way, when you do your checking, take abundant notes and save them. Start a file folder on each company you're interested in. And keep updating it as you go along.

You certainly know how to take notes and do research. You've been doing it all your life. This is the most important research you'll ever do.

As this book progresses, you'll see how to use and expand the notes you take to get and keep an upper hand throughout the rest of the game.

Taking all of this background checking seriously and going at it with dogged determination is well worth your time and effort. You'll have a competitive edge. And, as I said, you'll absolutely be able to handle any gaps in your own background by knowing how to position and fit yourself into currently available opportunities.

---

## HOW TO GAIN SECONDS

- Pick and choose only the parts of your background that relate to the job you want.

- Don't say anything negative about yourself.

- Notice that telling the truth works.

- Don't lie. Lying destroys your aliveness.

- Check out company backgrounds carefully. You can bet they'll be checking yours out.

- Do your research.

- Avoid blind box ads unless you can guess who's running them.

- Start a file folder on each company you're interested in.

- Be specific enough to make them want to create a position for you.

# 0:25
# Resume the Attack

Now that the strategy part is taken care of, you are ready to move into the next phase of getting your job. Your resume and your approach.

You probably realize that most people you know who are looking for jobs begin at this stage. That's precisely why they're looking for a job while you'll be getting one. According to your own game plan. In 60 seconds.

There are a lot of books around that tell you how to write your resume. It involves such an extraordinary combination of subjectivity and objectivity, though, that no one guide is ever completely right.

What I want to do, instead of giving you a line by line analysis, is to synthesize what each of the managerial, personnel and executive sources I spoke with had to say about the process. Complete with contradictions.

For example, one personnel director favors a freshly typed resume that's specifically oriented and tailored to the opening she's trying to fill.

Other personnel people find standard two-page formats acceptable if they're copied on a quality rag-content paper stock and don't look gray or mass-produced.

Still another corporate officer votes for a standard second page that lists details and a customized first page that clearly states how your qualifications and objectives specifically relate to his needs.

Allowing for vast differences of opinion, here's what you want to know about resumes.

Your resume is you in print. It needs to sound like you and look like you'll look when you follow it up in person. If your resume is dull and dry and conventional, lacking life and luster, and you're not like that at all, you haven't got it right yet.

Style is very important. And style has to fit a format. Just as you'll have to package yourself in the costume of the job territory, your resume style and content need to be packaged appropriately.

No stock format will totally fit your story. Resume formats are like fingerprints and eyes. No two living people have the same ones.

Format lengths range from one-page teasers to magazine-length treatises with accompanying color photos.

The truth is, at best, people read resumes the way they read newspapers. A quick glance at the front page taking in the lead paragraph. A few other paragraphs here or there. Seldom if ever turning to another page to finish the write-up.

However, if you've had more than two jobs, you'll definitely need two pages to cover your past performance and future goals. And no matter how many jobs you've had, more than two pages is much too much.

Use the format to demonstrate your uniqueness. Let it become a synthesis of your experience, talents, education and abilities.

My own last resume is either a very good or a very bad example of this. I intentionally broke all the rules with it, even my own. It's four pages long, professionally typeset and printed and too specific about details. It's also creative, stylish and slick. Even the rule-breaking part fits my personality. And it has been extremely well-received because it packages me perfectly in terms of the needs of my industry and my clients.

That's what you have to do. Be whoever you are. On paper.

Once you've determined the content, experiment with a layout that expresses who you really are. Play with visual presentation, capital letters, spacing, underlining and other devices to attract and hold the reader's attention.

But beware of letting your creativity dominate your message. Never let your form overpower your content.

Strictly for the record, here's the content you absolutely need to cover. In order of importance.

**Name**, address and telephone number at the top.

**Objective.** State what you intend to do on your next job. If your Job Game has a very broad objective, use this area to be specific and customize each resume you send. Avoid generalities like, "I want a good job I'll enjoy."

**Summary.** Condense your qualifications and any accomplishments that prove you can do what you say you want to do. Make this a clear, concise statement about your past contributions and how they empower your ability to contribute in the future. For example, how your managerial skills can save your next employer a lot of money, based on savings you created in the past. Or how your sales ability can produce a 14½ percent increase based on past performance.

**Experience and employers.** Put the most relevant first. According to prominent personnel directors, chronological order is no longer considered important. Start sentences with active verbs like Produced, Created, Organized, Directed. And tell just what you did at each job that made a difference there.

**Education.** List your highest degree first. Leave out secondary or lower education unless there is something extraordinary about it.

**Supporting data.** Include professional affiliations and awards that relate to the job you're after right now. Don't put down what you don't need to put down. Penmanship awards are out, unless you're applying for a position as a calligrapher. So is anything like a Masonic membership that might cause a conflict if your interviewer turns out be an Elk, a Moose, a Knight of Columbus or a Daughter of the American Revolution.

**Personal data.** When in doubt, forget it. When your age, health or marital status don't support your case, leave them out.

That's it. Unless you want to add a line that says "willing to relocate" or "supporting data will be available at interview." If you don't need to add one of those lines, don't.

To get it all together, write everything down on paper. From one to seven.

Then shorten what you wrote until it's clear, concise, imaginative and no more than two typewritten pages long.

Cut and keep cutting. Write and re-write. Get it all down in as few words as possible.

Then put enough time into playing with the format and the visual appearance until you're satisfied that you've expressed yourself as enthusiastically as you possibly can on paper.

Watch out for little things. "I got so annoyed reading a resume where the person used capital "I" instead of lowercase "l" to write the number "one" that I crumpled it up and chucked it out," says one company president.

Reminders about your resume:

Put your name and phone number at the top. Be sure you can be reached at that number.

Avoid qualifiers like "almost," "more than," "over." Don't weaken your presentation.

Use action verbs in your experience section. Start sentences with words like "Started," "Saved," "Produced," "Implemented."

Invent a descriptive title for yourself if the title of one of your prior positions doesn't adequately reflect what you really did. But don't lie. Just describe your working experience accurately.

Check your grammar and spelling.

Recheck your grammar and spelling.

Make sure your resume expresses the unique person you really are.

Now all that's left is to select your paper (white heavy bond works) and your copy or reproduction process (black rich-looking type works). "Mimeographed or gray copies don't make it," warns a national recruiter. "Each resume has to look as if it's your first time out. Happy. Fresh. Optimistic!"

When you've handled all that, you can zero in on your audience. You're almost ready to launch your attack.

Your audience consists of all the people you have been referred to by friends or associates with whom you shared your intention to get another job. It's also all the people in your field that you admire and would like to work for. Last but not least, it's all the ads you want to answer.

In each and every case, do not send your resume to a company or a person that you have not checked out for yourself. Remember that rule from the last chapter?

Here's why it's a rule.

Most resumes never get read or noticed because they go to the wrong people. The wrong people are the resume screeners in the personnel department, the secretaries who open the mail from blind ads and anyone else who is not the ultimate authority who can give you the job you want.

By studying the backgrounds of your companies and their management, you can pick and choose the ultimate authorities you want to reach. Maybe it won't always be the president or even a senior vice president. But it certainly won't be the new guy in personnel with 1,200 resumes on his desk.

You want to write to the ultimate authority each time you send out a resume. Or don't bother sending one out at all.

One unusually candid personnel interviewer says, "If you're answering a want ad, pretend that you're not. Instead of addressing your letter to the name on the advertisement, send it to the highest authority figure you can reach.

"Write your letter as if you didn't know anything about the ad. Write inquiring about the job you want, the position that fits your qualifications perfectly. Let it be seen as an enormous coincidence that your background makes you an ideal candidate for the advertised job.

"The authority you write to will be impressed. He'll eventually send your letter down to me with a personal note on it. The difference will be that it came to me from a very high place. It has significance.

"Letters that the postman or the secretaries bring in have no significance at all."

Do you get the point?

Your letter now has made a first impression that gets you a few more of the 60 seconds you need to get a job.

You've become a prime candidate for an interview. And when you show up later, you will have the implicit endorsement of someone in a very high place. You have become someone to be taken seriously. And you didn't get dropped into the round file with the rest of the bulk mail.

The whole idea is to be bold.

Take risks.

You can be safe and send your letter to Personnel. But you won't get the job in 60 seconds that way.

You can cover yourself and send two letters: one to the highest authority there and one to the Personnel Department, but the personnel people will catch on when the person you sent the first note to sends them a memo about you. After that, they'll figure you were going over their heads and they'll be out to sink you.

At this point if you're still on the fence you must choose. Keep on trying to get a job in the old traditional way. Or get one this way. In 60 seconds.

As for that letter, you know, the one that's going to produce incredible results. Here's how to handle that.

Be short and sweet. Be warm and friendly and emotionally involved. But be terse.

Don't be another "yours of the 14th" business letter.

A good rule for style is to write like you speak. If you can't read your letter out loud to a friend and have it sound like you, start again. Unless your conversation is always stiff and embarrassingly formal, tear up any letter that sounds that way. And write another.

Never, never, never misspell the name, use the wrong title, or guess the gender of your ultimate authority. And always address them by name. A "Dear sir or madam, whichever the case may be" will not get you what you want.

Most of the experts agree that your letter must cover, in as few words as posssible, the following:

Introduce yourself.

Tease and seduce the reader with something irresistably interesting about your background.

Present a clear understanding of your reader's business and mention a current problem that you are able to solve.

Offer more than just yourself. Offer some proven or potential experience.

Be original without being flaky.

Ask for an interview. Don't ask for a job. And don't even think of mentioning salary or salary levels. Get all that. It's essential.

Do all of the above in less than one page. Less than half a page is even better.

The experts generally do not agree about whether you should include your resume with your letter or not. So do whichever your research says will work.

If you do, you present a total picture of yourself. At this level, it may be overkill. If you don't, you leave some material for the interview. Just make sure you have covered your assets and qualifications for the job you want to get.

Another area of nonagreement is whether or not to use a reference or a referral's name as your door-opener.

Many decision-making executives want to know *who* you're coming from as well as where. However one corporate president says, "Sure I like to know how you got my name. But nine times out of ten, I'm skeptical. My automatic assumption is that the person who referred you isn't qualified to evaluate my personnel needs."

Actually the circumstances may be different each time you contact someone. After you've read your letter out loud to make sure it sounds like you, ask yourself: What else do I need to include to get an interview?

If your answer is nothing, fine. If it's a resume or anything else, also fine.

Either way, learn to recognize the fine line between overload and insufficient data. And give just enough to provoke your reader into absolutely needing to interview you to find out what makes you such an ideal candidate.

When that happens, you're rising above the first-impression level of initial contact on paper or over the phone with flying colors. And you're five more seconds ahead.

---

## HOW TO GAIN SECONDS

- Put name, address and phone number at top of your resume.
- Make certain that your resume is you in print.
- Keep all supporting data on your resume relevant, concise, and to the point.
- Check out *all* companies you send your resume to.
- Get your resume to the person who actually makes the decisions about hiring.
- Include a personal letter that tells how you can fill the needs and wants of the company.

# 0:30

# Homework Works

Remember that library work you did in 0:20? You pulled out all the published facts and figures you could find about the companies and the management of the companies you wanted to contact. You wrote down all those facts and figures. And you started file folders on each company.

That was only the beginning.

All of that information was above-the-ground data. Or information available to anyone who takes the trouble to look closely at the surface level of the Job Game reality.

Now that you're getting ready for that moment when you will make your in-person first impression, you need to dig below the surface. You need to hit pay dirt. Before you hit the interview.

Pay dirt contains everything about your next employer. It's all the dirt that the library material couldn't tell you.

In terms of actually getting your job, pay dirt is like pure gold. It's like buried treasure. It's like a deep layer of oil that will help you slide into your next paycheck. With a minimum of effort and friction.

Pay dirt includes specific answers you need to know about everything from what to wear to the interview to what your interviewer's favorite hobby is and whether or not it's a good idea to bring it up.

Pay dirt is homework that pays off. In the job you want.

It's homework you can't do in a library or in any other traditional way. It involves using all the imagination and intuition and courage you've got.

You have to keep finding new ways to do it. Because once you use the good old proven ways a few times, they won't work any more. In fact, once you lose the elements of innovation and surprise, you may actually hurt your chances of success. Instead of guaranteeing them.

First I'll tell you what kind of things you want to find out. Then I'll show you some of the ways other people have found out all those things in the past.

Your homework is to find answers to these questions. What's the company really like? How do you react emotionally to being there? What are the people like? What do they wear to work? What do they expect you to wear to your interview? How do they treat their employees? And how did their present employees get *their* jobs?

You also want to dig for information like this. Who's going to interview you? Will the interviewer be able to make the ultimate decision about your job? How long has he or she been at the company? Assuming it's a man, where did he work before? Where did he go to school? Where did he grow up? Where does he live now? What are his outside interests and hobbies? What is his personality like, his reputation, his role at the company? What kind of people does he hang around with? What kind of people does he hire?

You may not be able to find out all of it, although it's not that hard to do. The C.I.A. finds out all kinds of material like that and much more in minutes. So, without their resources, you can do it in a few hours of persistent questioning.

The more you know, the more time you get. And the closer you are to winning your Job Game in 60 seconds.

Here's why.

Whenever you can walk into an interview knowing who to expect, what to expect and how other people got hired there, your level of confidence will be genuinely higher. And the first impression they get of you will be clearer, cleaner and more positive than that of your unprepared competitors.

It's the difference in appearance between a Cheshire cat and a hungry cat. If you're the cat from Cheshire, you've just picked up five more seconds.

"People hire out of their own patterns and pictures," says the head of a national corporation.

"I tend to hire people who come to me looking for advice. I guess I like orphans and strays. All the key people I've brought in were asking for my expertise, asking for a favor. You get what you ask for. They got jobs at my company.

"By the way, I also have noticed that I hire women who wear sheer blouses and nylons. It plays out a favorite fantasy of mine.

"You could almost conclude that to get a job here, you need to ask me for advice or wear a sheer blouse. You wouldn't be far off."

By doing your homework you'd know all that. And you'd be sitting on the inside looking out instead of the other way around.

In a small company, pay dirt data-gathering is easiest. Your interviewer will always be one of the top-level people. Frequently it's even the president.

In a medium-sized company, start by finding out who the vice president in charge of your area is. Does he do his own interviewing? If not, who does?

In a large corporation, you'll probably want that same person, the VP in your field of interest. But sooner or later, you'll have to go through the Personnel Department to get your interview with him. So check to see exactly who in personnel will be handling your case. And find out all about him as well as the vice president you really want to see.

In all cases, go for the power source in decision making. Avoid people who are over the hill or about to retire. Their first impressions don't carry enough weight on the big scale of values upon which you are being measured.

So how do you do it?

How do you find out who's who and what the story is?

Lots of ways.

Even before you send your initial letter, you can call up and ask whose name ought to be on the envelope for best results. You might get a friendly and talkative ally on the other end who can tell you where the company seems to be heading and anything else you want to know.

"It's risky, but I'm usually impressed when someone brings their letter in themselves and asks me or my secretary to set an interview date on-the-spot. Of course, personal presentation becomes the deciding factor in this case," confides the vice president of a full-service bank.

In the process of doing your homework, anticipate when a company you are interested in is about to start hiring and get there before they place an ad. "I would have talked with someone for an hour or two just a couple of weeks before my last ad ran," says a graphic design firm's vice president. "When I had 145 replies to consider, each person I interviewed got less than fifteen minutes."

Obviously it's easier to get a job when you don't have to compete.

If you were turned down for a job in the past, don't be afraid to call the same company and ask again. "It's like asking for a date," advises a clothing wholesaler. "One 'No' doesn't mean anything personal. Jobs also break up from time to time just like relationships. So a company that's involved with someone else right now may be out looking around again next week."

A physical fitness center manager comments, "The last woman I hired as a racquetball instructor had sent me a resume in answer to an ad I ran and received no response.

"She dropped in one day and was turned away by the girl out front because the position had been filled.

"Then she came back to play and she just hung around until she could talk to me directly.

"I hired her instantly. We were just about to run another ad. When I think of all the time she saved us, I could give her a bonus. Maybe I will, but don't tell her that!"

All of which goes to show that intuitive contact, or listening to your impulses about when it's the right time to leap in, is one form of homework that produces results.

"It's much easier to do intensive research on a company than anyone thinks," says the personnel manager of a large financial services company. "Any candidate for a job could invent a variation of one of the techniques I use to find specialized people outside of the company.

"Not long ago, I was looking for a Spanish-speaking auditor and couldn't find one anywhere. I asked a friend in Miami to scout around and twenty-four hours later, he had lined up five of them.

"Here's how he did it. He called up a few of the largest companies in town and said, 'I just flew down from New York with a Spanish-speaking accounting fellow who said he works here and I can't remember his name. Can you tell me who I'm trying to call.'

"The receptionists and secretaries he spoke to were eager to cooperate and they rattled off more names than he could write down.

"The best of those names is working here right now."

Use the telephone.

Right now, you're not calling to line up your interview. You may even want to avoid using your real name. The idea with homework is not to get the job but to get everything else you need in order to get the job.

Be creative. Be outrageous. Be shameless. Protected by your anonymity you have nothing to lose but your lack of a job.

Call up and say you're an employment agency and you want to know what their specifications are. Tell them your service is free of charge and you have the perfect candidate for them.

Call up and say you're from a new trade magazine specializing in your field of interest. Get the names of all the department heads you want to see and their assistants so that you can send each one a free copy. Then call back and talk with each of their secretaries to fill out market-research questions on cards for free one-year trial subscriptions. Typical marketing questions for trade magazine subscribers include: Name of college and degree held. Length of service at company. Salary range. Home address. Marital data. Military service data. Hobbies and outside interests. Favorite sports and vacation places. Industry awards and association memberships.

Call up your college alumni office. Find out where other graduates have succeeded in your field. Get their names and titles, do your homework on them, contact them. Go and see them. You'll get the job.

Call up cold and say you have heard there is a new opening in your field. Or say "I understand you are about to advertise for a (name of job). I'd like to apply right now and save you all that time and expense!"

Calling up pays off.

According to a national recruiter, "I told one of my competitors about an opening with the first architectural firm I could think of, just to throw him off the track of the openings I was working on. He called up and placed five people there.

"There are more opportunities and openings than you or we can even imagine. Go to the source. Bust the system and you'll get the job. And don't be afraid to be brazen about system busting!"

The more specialized your field, the more it pays to call and ask questions. A nuclear power company manager notes that "The whole nuclear power industry is made up either of Navy people or degree people. Nuclear Navy people usually don't hire college degree engineers and vice versa. Find out where the people are most like you. Then go there.

"Also find out how you match up with the person who'll be interviewing you. People who remind me of me, I just naturally like something about them."

A corporate personnel interviewer recommends calling to "Find out which minorities are in this year." Then, if you are one of them, find out which companies are specifically looking for people of your minority group and apply there.

"Don't be afraid to speak up. If you have an Anglo-Saxon last name but your maiden name is Hispanic, be sure to let the interviewer know about it. Just about everybody is part minority. And women, by the way, can be a double minority.

"Minority groups are in great shape," she concludes. "The SBA even gives minority loans to people who can prove they're 1/64th Indian."

Still another recruiter agrees. "The office statistics show that more black and other minority engineers are getting placed right now than anyone else."

So calling up is one kind of homework that works.

Another kind is *going* there.

Stand outside in the parking lot and see who goes in and out some morning or evening.

Sit in the waiting room, if it's a large company, waiting for an appointment with someone who's not there. Call ahead and you can always come up with the name of someone who won't be there.

Your digging will tell you how much looking around is appropriate. If you're inventive, there are always ways to get in. Large companies sometimes offer tours. Take one the week before you have your interview. That's also the perfect time to ask questions.

When possible, drop off supporting material at your interviewer's office the day before your interview. Take relevant samples or your grade transcripts or the annual report of your present company with the story in it about how you raised sales by 15 percent.

Bring anything short of your high school yearbook.

Here's the payoff. You've impressed the interviewer by being highly organized. You've gotten a chance to talk to the secretary who can give you all sorts of information. And you showed yourself to everybody.

It all adds seconds. Which is exactly what you need to do at this point.

While you're there notice everything. What people wear. Whether it's three-piece suits or leather pants. How people respond to each other. How you react inside, just being in that environment.

Notice everything and you'll come up with an unbelievable amount of data and useful impressions.

Now, just in case you're a person who lives in Portland, Maine, and you want to get a job in Portland, Oregon, you can do much the same thing without actually doing it yourself. Call a friend or relative on the West Coast and get them to do that homework for you. Then phone them a week later for their results.

# Choices to Make about Jobs in Distant Locations

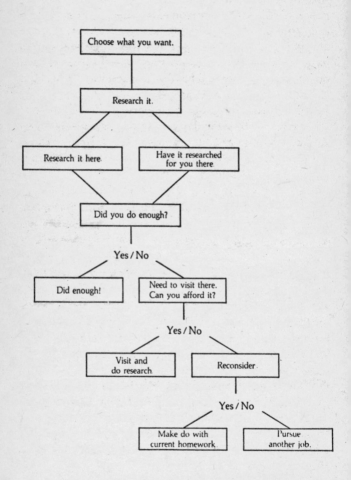

Discover your nearest resources for job information and then use them. Chances are you'll never have to be restricted by distance.

Another kind of homework that works is simple speaking up.

Tell everyone you meet, see and know that you're interested in the Farcas Corporation. Ask if anyone knows anyone who works there. Honestly, it won't be long before you've come up with the names of more Farcas Corporation employees than you'll need.

Then call them. Mention the name of the friend who referred you. And ask each one:

How they got their jobs.

How they like their jobs.

Who the interviewer you'll eventually see is likely to be.

Anything else you want to know.

People love to share stories if they're not too busy doing something else. So get as many stories as you can.

Keep good notes on everything. And keep building up your file on each company you expect to hear from for an interview. If you've been playing your Job Game at the 100 percent level, that should be each of the companies you've contacted so far.

By the time you actually get there, you'll know what to expect and whom to expect. And what is even more important, you'll know what each company needs and wants. Which will tell you exactly how to position yourself to make yourself the one candidate they can't afford to lose.

Homework works. It works spectacularly. It's worth at least five more seconds. And it might even be worth the whole game.

Do it diligently. Do it seriously. Do it completely. Do it.

---

## HOW TO GAIN SECONDS

- Dig below the surface for pay dirt.

- Do your homework. It doesn't get you the job, but it sure prepares you to get the job.

- Use all your advantages.

- Be creative in your attempts to gain information.

- Know what the company needs and wants and provide it.

# 0:35

# On the Spot

The personnel manager of a major corporation tells how he first went to work for his company:

"I had been laid off and I had a growing family and very little professional experience. One day I got a call from an employment agency. A personnel department job had just come in on a listing. Was I interested? Sure was.

"In spite of my eagerness and my financial urgency, I had the interview date set a week away and I went to work. I found out all about the company at the library. How it got to be so big. What each of its branches and satellite companies did. The names and stories about all the key corporate officers. Where the company was headed and what some of the upcoming problems and obstacles to growth appeared to be.

"Then I told everyone I knew that I was going for an important interview and I asked whether anyone knew any of the personnel people there. Turned out that one friend was a cocktail party acquaintance of the man who had the job I have now, the man I was most likely to see when I showed up at my appointment.

"I found out all I could about him. What he wore to parties, what he talked about, what he looked like and what his interests were.

"For instance, I knew he was an expert on the history of trains. And that if I brought up the subject of railroads, the interview would become hopelessly sidetracked.

"Even as well-armed as I was with information, when I drove up to the company parking area I was really scared. The size of the building and the massiveness of the corporate structure were overwhelming. The only reason I can remember for going through with the interview was that I had already spent two dollars for gas and I didn't want to waste the money.

"When I saw the receptionist and the secretary, I memorized their names. I used their names in casual conversation before the interview. And I thanked one of them personally later on when she brought some coffee in.

"The moment I saw my interviewer, I knew my sources were correct. I was wearing the same colored suit and tie that he was. I had brought all the right samples. My questions showed that I had a remarkable understanding of the company's present status and of the criteria for the job I wanted and this more than made up for my lack of experience in the field. I didn't mention trains.

"I got the job notification the next day. Both the receptionist and the secretary had put in a good word for me.

"The most interesting thing of all was I knew I had that job less than thirty seconds after I walked into the interviewer's office!"

That's how it's supposed to work. And if you've done all your homework, that's how it will work for you.

Since the interview contains all the critical mass of your Job Game, this and the next two chapters analyze, dissect and clarify the issues involved. They lay out the plans and procedures that will propel you into your next position.

All of this material is valid whether you are applying for a job at a small company where only one person interviews you or whether you're being led through a series of interviews at a giant corporation. At each stage in the series simply take it from the top, knowing that each time you are one step closer than you were before.

The first part of the process includes being and feeling as if you're on the spot. Totally and completely on the spot. Or acknowledging to yourself precisely where you are internally as well as externally.

To be on the spot and to perform successfully, you need to have handled as many of the known variables as you can. So that you can be alert and ready for anything unexpected.

Step back for a moment and consider what that means.

Before you get anywhere near your interview, consider the following points. Corporate vice presidents and personnel people agree with them. As one puts it, "You've got to psyche up.

"Start by reviewing everything you've written down about the company you're going to see. It's easiest when you've been using separate file folders for each company you've been researching.

"In your review, check for the latest corporate news, the material that will be most active on the top-of-mind awareness level of your interviewer.

"Test your memory on the names and titles of key management people and officers.

"Review the answers you've prepared for every question that could come up, just like politicians do before news conferences. That way you won't have to ad-lib. Ad-libbing invariably gets you in trouble.

"Select the questions you'll want to ask when your interviewer offers you that opportunity. (We'll cover the issues of questions and answers in the next chapter.)

"Run through all the data and all the events that led to you getting the interview in the first place.

"Finally, never be late. In fact, get there early.

"If you're lucky, you'll be able to engage the receptionist or a secretary in a conversation. You might be able to find out about your competition or how the interviewing has been progressing in terms of quantity and quality.

"You'll certainly have a chance to be in the flow of corporate activity and get a feeling for what it might be like to work there. You won't be crashing in cold."

By now you know what to wear. You found out when you did your homework and took a trip to the company parking lot or reception room. Or from the advice of a friend who works there, or who referred you to someone who did.

Just in case you're not clear about that, the idea is to look and dress like your interviewer. In most job categories, your interviewer will look and dress like your own picture of conformity. The notable exceptions are jobs in the arts, creative departments, entertainment field, physical fitness activities, small stores and fast food counters.

In several different types of jobs, what you wear to the interview will be quite different than what you will wear to work. Don't get the two confused. First you have to get the job. And one way to get the job is to fit the interviewer's picture of what a well-dressed employee looks like. This is particularly true for many jobs in industry and service fields. But it's also true on many corporate levels where you might be able to out-style and out-class your interviewer, only to lose his or her vote.

A strong consensus of people who have the heaviest vote about hiring other people told me that they favor the following dress codes.

A man in a dark or light-colored conservative suit, white shirt, tie, long dark socks, well-shined shoes and no conspicuous jewelry.

A woman in a dark, below-the-knee skirt-suit, light coordinated blouse, full-cut long-sleeved jacket and conservative makeup and hair styling.

"People who wear white shirts get jobs," says one personnel department supervisor, "others don't. It's like being in a fancy restaurant and having your meal brought out in a brown paper bag."

The personnel director for a large, well-known insurance company says, "We hire a lot of kids right out of college. So we continually get a phenomenon around here called 'The Interview Suit'.

"What it is, is the first suit, shirt and tie a kid has had on in four years. It doesn't always look like it fits or coordinates properly, and the person in it looks and acts uncomfortable as hell.

Some of my interviewers take points off for that. They think it looks tacky. I don't. I take it as a sign of growth and I like it.

"I'd recommend though, that all younger applicants or anyone that this applies to should wear their interview clothes at least long enough to feel comfortable in them. Before they get to the interview."

Check your personal grooming carefully. Dirty fingernails will cost you the job. So will bad breath, rings around the collar and all the other things the TV commercials warn you against.

Another personnel manager says, "My favorite spot check is the three Hs: hair, hands and heels. One negative H and you're out."

Now that you know that someone might even notice the condition of your heels, you'd better notice it too.

Bring a pocket dictionary with you in case something comes up on the application that you don't know how to spell. "A woman who interviewed with us had a master's degree in psychology. She spelled it wrong when she wrote it down," confided still another personnel manager. "She didn't get the job."

Also bring with you a few extra copies of your resume and any supporting material that demonstrates your capabilities.

For instance, if you're a writer looking for a job, don't forget to bring samples of your work.

Wherever you go, have a clean pad of paper handy. You'll want to copy down the exact name and title of your interviewer and you'll need it for note-taking, especially during the latter part of your interview. (More on this later.)

Finally, on the day of your interview, even though you are involved in all these details and loose ends, keep your morning routine constant.

If you enjoy a big breakfast, have a big breakfast. If you never eat until lunch, don't eat until lunch. If you run every morning or meditate or pray or do yoga or exercises, do those things. If you don't, don't.

Allow enough time to take care of yourself. All of the things that get your day off to a well-centered beginning are things you need to do the day of your interview. In other words, do everything you ordinarily do, just the way you ordinarily to it. That way, you are giving a major and potentially stressful event a stable, solid base.

So now you're back on the spot.

You're dressed appropriately, you know your material and you're sitting in their waiting room, waiting and looking around.

In the time you have left, you want to check and see if your aliveness and enthusiasm are in high gear.

Remember how important aliveness and enthusiasm are? Here's how to create them along with a supersharp level of awareness and a heightened mental acuity, any time and any place.

Just exhale all your breath, every bit of it. Then inhale as much new air as you can and hold it all in for at least thirty seconds. Hold it longer if possible.

That's all.

When you exhale again and resume your normal breathing patterns, you'll notice a tingling sensation throughout your body and a higher degree of mental alertness than you had before. (Try it now and see how well it works.)

When the secretary comes to escort you to your interview room ask her where you can leave your coat and any unnecessary articles. You want to walk in with just your self and the few supportive materials you need.

Then scan yourself and notice whatever is going on internally. Notice it accurately and completely between now and the time you shake hands with your interviewer and sit down again.

As you scan yourself, quickly run through each of the following areas.

Check your body sensations. Notice where you feel tense and where you don't feel anything at all. Notice your breathing. Are you breathing?

Check your emotions. How do you feel? Give it a word. Scared. Petrified. Confident. Excited. Nervous. Quickly tell your self that everything is OK just the way it is and that you love feeling the way you feel, whatever that is. This is important. Don't ignore your feelings. If you don't accept the way you're feeling right now, honestly and truly, even if you're cold-sweat panicked, you'll blow your first impression.

Check your thoughts. All that activity in your head that sounds like a voice-over is your thoughts. Notice everything that little voice in there is telling you. About the secretary, how she looks, who the interviewer reminds you of and whether you like that or not. Notice all your business about looking good, failing, the times you failed in the past, success and how you really may be afraid to succeed. All that stuff is thoughts. Let all those thoughts be there and also notice their lack of substance. Notice that they don't mean anything. And notice how that's true.

Check your attitudes about the interviewer. If you've done your homework, who your interviewer is won't come as a complete surprise. But whether you've done your homework or not, be sure to connect with this fact: Your interviewer reminds you in some way of someone you have known in the past and, as a result, you have a thought that either you like the interviewer or you don't.

So ask yourself if the interviewer is really that person or not. And whether any of this means anything. Finally, take the time to notice that your interviewer is doing the same thing with you. And that the whole process happens automatically and almost instantaneously.

If you've cleared yourself this much, without doing anything else, you'll be relaxed and open and alive. Your interviewer will decide that he likes you and wants you in the company.

Bingo! You've just won five more seconds.

Now you need to shift your focus away from yourself. You've handled yourself if you followed this procedure.

Look around the room you're in and notice what's unusual about it. Something always is. If nothing seems unusual, that's unusual. So notice that.

"If someone doesn't notice and react to the stuffed elephant in the corner of my office or do a double-take when my clock begins to talk," says a successful publisher, "then I don't want them on my staff. I want people here who are aware of where they are and alive enough to enjoy it all.

"I also want them to stop and look and ask questions when I take them on a tour. Genuinely. Not merely going through the motions. It's the same principle of reacting to and enjoying where you are."

At this point the introductions and warm-up period are over. The interview is starting in earnest.

If your attention is off yourself as it needs to be by now, you'll know how to work with the questions.

Actually, there are only two kinds of interviewers. After reading this, you'll know one from the other and how to act accordingly.

"I consider people who let me do most of the talking to be the most knowledgeable," says a representative from the first group. "People who try to impress me lose. I want them to be responsive, not assertive. Just answer fully and leave out the details."

"Most applicants dread interviews," claims a vice president who falls into the second group. "They hold back and wait for questions. They have no questions of their own. They make me do all the work. To get a job here, you have to engage me and participate with me."

Either way, give some thought to this advice from people who make their living interviewing and hiring other people.

"Be the type of person you'd want to hire yourself if you were the interviewer."

"Talk to the interviewer as if she were a friend and not a rigid authority figure."

"Always be who you are. Don't be different when you're at an interview. Tell the truth about what you're really like. Otherwise, after you get the job you might not like it."

"Watch what your hands are doing."

"Remember you're not talking uphill to management. It's like a partnership and you're both on equal levels."

"Get the chip off your shoulder. We're currently leaning over backwards to hire women for a job category that used to be men only. One young woman mentioned that she had had a summer job in college as a typist. Automatically, I said 'Oh, you can type!' Just as automatically, she let me have it. 'I didn't come here for a typing job!' Then she got up and stormed out of my office. Too bad. She was well-qualified. And she did not get the job."

"Don't try to impress me. One kid walked in for an interview with a *Wall Street Journal* under his arm and he proceeded to read it while I was talking to him! Another, applying for an auditing position, confided coolly that he had been around long enough to know that even in insurance 'there was a quick way to turn a dollar!' Forget it!"

"If you're a Chevy with an AM-FM radio, white walls, and 20 MPG, don't try to present yourself as a Mercedes Benz, an Alfa Romeo or a Jeep."

In general, maintain an automatic monitor on your aliveness and enthusiasm. When they start to fade, notice it. And turn on more juice. If they continue to fade, notice that. Maybe you are trying to get the wrong job. Or maybe something is going on that requires your immediate attention.

Whenever your natural aliveness keeps fading into unconsciousness, there's something up that part of you doesn't want to know about. You can't afford to have that happen when you're at your interview. Find out what it is. Quick.

Other than that, there are only three varieties of mistakes that have serious enough consequences to cost you the extra seconds of time for which you've been working.

The first is you don't hear a question because your attention wandered back inside instead of staying 100 percent outside, where it belongs.

The second is you give an answer that wasn't asked for or needed, one that throws unnecessary material into the room.

The third is you try to ad-lib and answer a question off the top of your head. Not doing that is so important that it's worth five seconds all by itself.

So the next chapter will tell you how to go for all five of those seconds. And get them.

---

## HOW TO GAIN SECONDS

- Get to the interview early.
- Dress like your interviewer dresses.
- Wear your interview suit at least once before you go to the interview.
- Bring any relevant material that supports you as the best candidate for the job.
- Wear a watch and bring a pen.
- Don't answer questions that weren't asked. Don't ad-lib.
- Know the company as completely as you can. Know its problems and its opportunities.

# 0:40

# Questions, Questions

Questions in an interview are like questions on an examination. They're never too hard when you've prepared your material in advance. You need to know what your answer will be to any question that could conceivably come up.

I touched on this in the last chapter. And it's worth noting again. Every politician from the mayor of your town to the president of the United States does this before attending a press conference: they memorize a prepared set of answers to all the questions their aides and advisors can think up and prepare on a list.

As a result, the delivery of each answer is smooth and inspires confidence. You never become aware of any slips, emotional flare-ups or loss of enthusiasm or significance. And you never will, because it's all so carefully rehearsed. Each line has been learned as well as any actor's.

You can do the same thing now. In this practice interview just use the questions I've synthesized from interviews with fifty-six professional personnel people, corporate officers, managers, department heads and job givers on every level.

Use this chapter to note which questions apply to you and your current Job Game.

Then prepare a two-to-four-sentence answer to each question. Two to four sentences are all you need. Occasionally two to four words will do. Keep your answers short and sweet. But whatever you do, answer these questions now.

Then learn your answers so well that each of them becomes a part of you and not something you just memorized. Having the answers, in other words, isn't enough. Actually becoming and being the answers will get you the job.

Practice your answers in front of a mirror and notice what you are doing as you say the words.

, "I always watch a candidate's eyes and body movements, knowing that mental tension and unrest often express themselves in unconscious movements. A person's body language usually speaks louder than words," says one personnel manager for a regional retail chain.

"Sometimes I don't even listen to answers. I watch the eyes instead."

With each question, I'll suggest guidelines for answers that interviewers claim can earn you extra points and extra seconds. If you don't think the suggestions will work for you, don't use them. Make up your own instead.

Just be sure you don't skim over anything in this section. And don't leave anything out. The questions you don't prepare answers for now are the questions that will trip you up later. Count on it.

## Standard Questions

Why do you want to change jobs? Stay away from reasons like money, prestige, personality problems with your boss and boredom. Have a grand and glorious reason that makes sense.

Why should I hire you? Summarize in one sentence or less how you meet the company's current needs.

What makes you think this job is any different than all your other jobs? Find an answer that offers some certainty that you are more than a job jumper who's poised and ready for still another leap. Tell how you are committed to that answer.

Why do you want to work here? Remember your homework and pinpoint why you and the company are a perfect match.

What interests you most about this job? Keep the pace alive by coming up with a two-to-four-word answer. Like The Growth or The Opportunity or the New NASA Contract. Occasional short volleys keep the energy up.

What contributions have you made to sales or profits or cost efficiencies or whatever? Don't assume anyone read your resume. Condense a few success stories. Be sure you communicate your story clearly. And don't confuse your answer by blowing your own horn.

Would you like your supervisor's job? Never say no.

Would you be willing to relocate? Again, never say no. Handle the problem later. With finesse, you'll never have to move anywhere that you don't want to be. Besides, willingness to relocate and actually relocating are miles apart.

Who has been the most unforgettable influence in your life? Make it a short but appropriate story. Cover who, what, where, when, why and how, quickly, like a good newspaper reporter.

What causes you to lose your temper? Keep it innocuous. Other people's repeated latenesses or lazyness are acceptable. Avoid anything heavy.

How's your health? Tell the truth without going overboard. Give assurance that any problems are safely in the past.

What do you want to be doing ten years from now? Use your homework to fit your personal objectives into the framework of the company's objectives.

What kinds of decisions do you have difficulty making? Keep your answer light. It's another area where being innocuous pays off.

Why aren't you earning more money? Don't get rattled. And don't talk about salary. If you've been investing in your own skills, learning, talent and potential, say so.

How do you feel about your progress so far? Don't complain and don't knock it.

Do you intend to continue your education? Know whether the job requires another degree level and answer accordingly.

What are your most outstanding achievements? Present another short summary from your resume. Maybe they missed the point. Make sure they get the point now.

Which of your qualifications best fits our needs? Your homework will tell you the answer. Your answer will reveal exactly how much you know about the company's real position in the market.

How will you like working for a male/female supervisor? If it makes any difference to you either way, you've just blown it.

How long can I count on you to stay here if I hire you? Make it conditionally open-ended, or as long as growth opportunities and challenges remain available to you. Your homework will clue you in on what you want from them.

Is there any way you would like to change anything that you've said? Take this opportunity to clarify anything you think you need to restate, or to add anything you forgot.

What salary level do you expect? Don't talk dollars yet; it's not the right time. Say that you'd like to know more about the job before you assign a dollar value to it.

## Specialized Questions

How many people have you supervised? If you never have, say so. But tell how you managed the department when your boss was on vacation or whatever else you did that qualifies as supervision.

Does your present employer know you're looking? You're in a better bargaining position, if your answer is no. That way your interviewer has to work to steal you away. And you won't be a pushover for a low-end-of-the-scale salary.

Have you ever hired or fired anyone? If you haven't, find a good one-sentence answer that shows you're capable of evaluating people and dealing fairly with them.

Why have you changed jobs so often? Prepare a reasonable answer. Add a note to reassure your interviewer that you've jumped your job for the last time and finally plan to settle in.

Why were you out of work so long? Dig for the reason that makes you look good. Maybe you've been taking some courses or organizing your life differently or waiting for the right opportunity. Pick an answer that you would believe if someone else told it to you.

But you don't have... Cover missing qualifications by acknowledging that it's true. Quickly point out what you do have that compensates completely for each gap.

What are your present salary requirements? Keep fencing. It's still too soon to talk about money. Say that once you know you are right for this job you can talk about your salary more knowledgeably.

## Trick Questions

Aren't you a little old/young for this job? Tell how your age and experience or your youth and enthusiasm make you the perfect candidate.

Don't you think you're overqualified for this level of work? Same story. It's another opportunity to turn a concern into an asset. All your interviewer wants from you is some assurance that if you are hired, you won't make the interviewer look wrong in the eyes of his or her own boss.

So you didn't like your last job (long pause)... Many people can't stand silence. They'll jump in and say anything. Don't be one of them. Use silence and long pauses as a chance to take a deep breath or two.

What time is it? They want to see whether you have a watch and what kind of watch it is.

Would you sign this? They want to see if you brought a pen.

Would you please open that window? If it's nailed down, they want to see whether they can rattle you under pressure. Don't get rattled by childish tricks like this. Volley them back by telling the truth about how the window feels as if it's nailed shut.

What do you think of that, Thelma? Your name is Harriet. Did you get flustered? Don't. If there were no tricks, the game would get boring very quickly. Gently correct the interviewer and answer the question.

Have you done the best work you're capable of doing? The answer had better be a qualified yes. Don't evaluate yourself out of a job.

All of us enjoy a good game of tennis. Do you? If you don't, don't lie. Reassure your interviewer that you don't intend to make your appearance on the job as a social outcast.

Can you sell me this penholder on my desk? The trick is to take your time. Don't jump right in selling. Ask questions about the penholder. You can't sell anything you don't know about. When you know what your interviewer likes about the penholder, feed him back each point as you build your sales case. You'll not only sell the penholder. You'll be selling yourself.

What do you expect to earn on this job? Keep dodging the question. It's still too soon to talk about money.

## Dirty and Otherwise Illegal Questions

All of these questions do not require answers. They are illegal and should not be asked. However, things being as they are, sometimes an interviewer will ask you some of them anyway. Getting upset or calling in a lawyer won't get you the job. The best advice is to use your judgment. If you notice an unusual amount of concern behind an illegal question and if it doesn't bother you too much to disclose the information, volunteer just enough data to enable the interviewer to shift to another subject. If your interviewer keeps pushing one of these subjects, you have to decide if this is the type of place where you want to work.

How old are you?

How much do you weigh?

Are you married or engaged?

Who lives with you?

How old are your children?

Do you plan to have more children?

Who'll take care of the children while you're at work?

How are you getting along with your ex?

Do you rent or own your home?

What's the story on your military background?

Do you have a criminal record?

## First Time Questions

What's your Grade Point Average? Support your GPA with contributions you made working your way through school.

What courses did you like best? Long before now, you should have examined the suitability of the courses you took. If you didn't like the courses that relate to the job, you might be applying for the wrong job.

What honors have you achieved? Summarize what's on your resume. Be brief.

Which school activities were you involved in? Be relevant. The debating team might give you an edge for a sales or law office job. The track team won't. Unless, of course, your interviewer is a serious jogger or a marathon runner. If you've done your homework, you'll know.

How would your best friend describe you? Keep it to a single sentence and make it count. Depending on the nature of the job you're after, answers like "Sort of a grind when there's work to be done," or "Able to sell ice chests to Santa's elves" are both on target.

What books have you read in the last few weeks? What plays or movies have you seen? Know which ones in advance. Make sure they strengthen your cause.

Why do you want to be in this field? Use your homework to form a link between what you like about your chosen area of work and the company's contributions in that area.

How long do you think it will be before you can make a contribution to our firm? Whiz kid answers are inappropriate. Learning, training, experience and time are the ingredients from which meaningful contributions are made. Be conservative, but be positive.

## Heavy Questions

What will you do if your boss makes a counter offer? Acknowledge that it's likely. And that you are firmly committed to making a more suitable move and why that's so.

What do you want out of life anyway? If you say you want money or position or power, you lose ground. It's not even the truth. The bottom line is that all everyone ever wants to do is to make a contribution, to share themselves and their abilities and to make a difference in their environment. What you want to communicate is that you want intrinsic motivation like job satisfaction, not extrinsic motivation like money. Find a three-sentence version of all that and use it.

Why didn't you accomplish more? Go to graduate school? Become a supervisor? Look and see whatever it is you are most embarrassed about not having done and prepare a positive, upbeat answer about why you didn't do it. Keep your answer to two sentences. There's no need to run yourself down.

Can you start next week? A relieved "yes" will demonstrate that you are unreliable and cost you the job.

Be fair to your present boss if you are employed. Also be fair to yourself and give yourself time to wrap up any loose ends and find out about other pending offers. You can start your new job as soon as you clean up your current act. Estimate how long that will take and let the interviewer know.

Do you have any questions? Expect the ball to come your way at any time. And be ready. If that doesn't happen, make it a point to ask whether you can toss out a few questions of your own. Otherwise you create the impression of being much too passive, dull, wimpy and boring to be considered seriously.

Good questions earn you valuable seconds toward your getting-the-job-in-60-seconds goal. Good questions will also help you determine whether or not you want the job after you get it.

Add any specific or pressing questions of your own to the following basic list. Each time you ask another question, have your notebook handy and jot down the answers you get.

You need to have a record of each answer to keep your file complete, to follow up on later and to use after you get the job.

If taking notes rattles your interviewer, let that be all right. At this particular moment, you have more at stake that he or she does.

While you're taking notes, keep the conversation flowing. Don't keep the interviewer waiting. Always look up when you ask your questions and make eye contact.

Ask questions like these.

Why is this job available?

Why isn't this job being filled from inside?

How many people have had this job in the last five years?

Could I speak with the person who had this job most recently?

What happened to that person anyway?

What new skills will I learn here?

How many people are you interviewing?

Where does this job fit into the organizational structure?

Can I see a corporate chart?

Exactly what will you expect from me in this job?

What kind of results have been produced in this job so far?

How many people will report to me?

How is their performance?

How does their salary level compare with industry averages?

What will I have to do to earn a promotion?

What is this company's major problem right now?

How do you like *your* job?

What do you like least about working here?

How soon will you know if you are going to hire me?

Do you have any questions or concerns about my background, my qualifications or anything I've told you so far?

Obviously that last question returns the ball to your interviewer. And it gives you a chance to take care of anything that has not been clearly communicated so far.

At this point, the interview will shift to another level. When that happens, you will be five more seconds ahead.

---

## HOW TO GAIN SECONDS

- Review the questions you're likely to be asked before the interview.
- Learn your answers so well they become a part of you.
- Practice your answers in front of a mirror.
- Prepare a list of your own questions.
- Take notes when your interviewer answers you.
- Avoid discussing salary.

# 0:45
# Money Talks and Other Issues

How do you know when you're about to get an offer?

Watch for a shift in the atmosphere of the room. Tensions will relax. You'll sense a change in attitude.

"Whenever an interview lasts longer than thirty minutes, I'm close to making an offer," says a sales executive. "I have my day all blocked out into half-hour time slots, and I seldom change my schedule. I don't like being late. I don't believe in wasting time. So someone has to be fairly special to go into overtime."

"When I'm ready to take the applicant to meet his potential supervisor or other people in the company, I've already given him my vote," notes the personnel manager of a regional chain of restaurants.

"I know I'm hooked when I start to sell harder," says the personnel director of a large corporation.

"When I take an applicant on a quick tour of the place, I know I like them. Then, if they make the walk-around interesting for me by asking questions or making comments, I'm really sold," reveals an advertising agency vice president.

"If I'm really interested in someone, I'll have checked her out by the time I meet her. I'll know more about her than the resume or the interview has brought to light. Towards the end of the interview, I'll begin to sum up why I want that particular person working here, and I'll throw in some of the extra material I learned on my own," confides the owner of a weight-loss center for women. "That happens just before I make my offer."

When you notice any signs like these, settle back in your chair and zip up your lip. If you talk too much when you ought to be listening, you'll be subtracting seconds that you may never have a chance to recover.

Wait until this positive shift in your favor, if it's at all possible, before you begin to talk about salary.

If you disclose your figure before this point in the interview, you'll be stuck with it. And if you have either seriously undersold or overpriced yourself, it's all over.

Bide your time. Keep fencing about money. Don't discuss it until you begin to get the idea that they've bought your basic suitability and they want you to take the job.

At that point, you don't have to be a highly trained negotiator to get what you know you're worth.

It's all based on this model of simplicity. Know what your interviewer wants and needs and stay on target.

Keep emphasizing only those qualifications and accomplishments that relate to those wants and needs. And make a forceful and confident statement that you can do the job because your capabilities perfectly match their requirements.

If you can handle that, you'll be in great shape at this stage of your Job Game.

"Any candidate's salary offer is based on three variables," says a computer company officer. "How confident of his value he really is and how well he communicated that confidence. How he fits into my available income range and structure. And how good he is at reading my mind."

If you've done your homework, those three variables won't be a problem at all. Neither will the following:

What the job description pays on an industry-wide and a regional basis.

What a reasonable salary increase is in your field.

What your own value to the industry is, using strictly objective criteria.

The president of a national recruiting firm advises, "Don't be too greedy or expect too big a jump. In the high-tech field, you could expect a 20 to 25 percent increase but not more than that.

"I encourage my people to tell the truth about what they're getting paid now. You don't want to work for anyone who will use your present salary as a base and only offer you 10 percent more. That's cheap and small-time.

"Leave the salary box open on applications. And don't be afraid to preface a salary discussion with a statement like: 'I want a financial incentive to leave my job.' Or 'I want my contribution to be fairly compensated.'

"Use whatever means are available to you including acting skills to avoid coming from a position of scarcity or survival. Sweaty hands don't win.

"Know when they want you. When they do, you don't have to oversell or overkill. Just let them seduce you."

"If homes were sold the way jobs are negotiated," says the personnel manager of an insurance company, "we'd want to know what you paid for your house before we made you an offer.

"And by the way, I make it a rule to always reject an applicant whose only reason for changing jobs is money. I don't want to be responsible for justifying anyone's position in the marketplace."

Still more advice, and an altogether different point of view about money discussions, comes from a manufacturing company's personnel interviewer. "Very few people actually understand this, but there is a world of difference between going to an interview and making a commitment to change your job. Don't use my name but you can tell your readers they can use their interviews to assist them in gathering up-to-the-minute comparative data about their net worth in the marketplace relative to everyone else's.

"This is especially valuable in terms of striking exactly the right balance between your salary and your experience."

In other words, part of your research about how much you can expect to be paid by your next employer can come from interviews you set up strictly for practice.

It's an interesting concept. Practice interviews can be just like dress rehearsals. You might try one to fine-tune your answers to questions or work on your ability to maintain a condition of aliveness. You need to try one if you haven't figured out your next bottom-line salary minimum.

Practice interviews can range from going to people in your field for advice to actually pursuing job interviews. Either way will show you how to put this book into practice before the real thing.

But get all your practicing done long before you show up for your important job interviews. You know, the ones for the jobs you really want to crack wide open.

So imagine that you're back with your interviewer again. This time let's assume it's a woman. The shift has happened. You're feeling confident. And you're laying back a little.

Ideally she'll bring up the issue of your salary before you do. When that happens, you know she's decided you're the right person for the job. So far.

And that puts you in the perfect position for negotiation.

"I always have a starting figure in mind," says one personnel manager, "as well as my range upward. I know exactly what I have to work with.

"If the candidate throws a figure at me, my assumption is always that it is his maximum salary fantasy, so I'll undercut it by as much as I can.

"If that first figure is out of range, the interview breaks down all together."

That's why it's a smart tactic to let the interviewer mention a potential salary first. If your interviewer is being cagey and waiting for you to go first, here are a few ways to turn the tables on her.

Ask blatantly just what figure she had in mind.

Ask what the salary spread that she has looks like.

Or get her agreement on what the job will be worth in a couple of years when you have proven yourself. And then ask for a reasonable starting salary based on that.

Keep working toward a proposed salary based on your value to the company and not on your present financial needs.

Eventually, your interviewer will put a salary offer on the table and nudge it over to you. If you sit tight without being irritating or difficult, it is inevitable. After all, the interviewer needs to keep the interview moving along. That's her job. And negotiating your salary is a big part of her job.

When you get an offer, keep your cool. Pretend you're playing poker and don't let any trace of emotion go to your head or your face.

"When I see a thoughtful silence," says the personnel head of a national package goods corporation, "I know the applicant is considering my offer and that he isn't sold on it. It's like nonverbal communication. No answer tells me no acceptance.

"I'll usually go to my next level without any further discussion. It's just good business to do that. And besides, I've still left myself plenty of room."

The idea is to be totally enthusiastic about the job and thoughtfully concerned about the modesty of the salary offer.

When everyone at the interview wants a successful resolution, the old sales training cliche holds true. Whoever talks last, wins.

It may take more than one session to resolve your salary. Keep your aliveness up and don't worry. After all, that second trip back may be worth a few thousand dollars or more. That's not so bad.

Don't lose your confidence in yourself. You won't as long as you stick to the rules of your Job Game and keep remembering that since it's your game, you're the one who keeps creating it the way it is.

Even if you are out of work, a confident point of view and a realistic sense of your value to your next employer will maintain your ability to bargain effectively.

A few more pointers from professional personnel department executives:

"When you know your salary range in the market is $30,000 to $35,000, for example, always ask for the higher figure. If you ask for the range, I know you'll settle for the bottom end and I'll get to save the company $5000 a year."

"Whenever I offer a range to see what will happen, the response I respect most is the one that repeats the top figure back to me and tells me 'that would be a good place to start talking from.' "

Part of the trick here is to have done your homework. Know what similar positions pay at other companies. Then aim a little higher. Give yourself room to negotiate.

By the way, make sure you do know the salary before you leave the room. Some people actually accept and start new jobs without knowing what they'll be paid.

"Don't get lost in salary discussions and forget about fringe benefits. After you agree to a figure, you can always add volume to the package by getting me to commit to the fringe benefits available here."

As part of your homework, be sure you have looked into fringes. In many industries, fringe benefits can be worth 25 percent of your salary or even more.

Employers that I spoke to offer everything from free lunch (at a fast food restaurant counter job) to cars, medical and dental insurance, profit sharing, deferred retirement income, credit cards and housing. One medical equipment company even sends its employees on expense-paid bonus vacation trips to Mexico or the Caribbean every Christmas.

Wherever you get your job, make sure you also get your share of the extras. When you know exactly what to ask for, you'll find very little resistance.

In a few cases, once the salary and terms are agreed to, you may receive your job offer immediately. If you do, congratulate yourself for winning your Job Game in well under 60 seconds.

More times than not, you've still got a ways to go.

Before you leave your interview, you need to make sure that no uncovered details are left behind to trip you up later. You may even want to handle one or more of the illegal areas of questioning that came up earlier.

For instance, if you are a single parent and you sense that your interviewer feels a little uneasy about not being able to talk to you about that, you might simply tell her what she needs to know. Tell her who'll be taking care of the kids while you're working, how your mother lives in, that you have a two-year-old car that's in great shape and that you were never late or absent from your last job because of the children.

Or if you sense that there is some vague or undelivered question about how you and your last boss got along, bring it up yourself and talk briefly about it, just to lay the issue to rest. Say that you want the interviewer to be completely assured that, even though you and your boss had a personality conflict, it never got in the way of your work. In fact, you handled all the projects with ease (name them again) and produced terrific results.

There's some lack of agreement about whether or not you should ask for a written job offer or written confirmation of the salary offer.

You take a chance by asking. The interviewer might think you're organized, efficient and conscious of details. Or the interviewer might think you're going to be a disagreeable troublemaker. It's probably not worth it.

The written offer isn't much legal protection. The job description could be changed. The salary could be reduced. If you feel as if you need the written offer, and they're not interested in giving it, it's probably not the type of place for you. Remember, it's just another detail.

When everything else is going your way, concede the details. Petty details don't matter at all. Getting the job matters. Play it that way.

And remember, it's never too late to blow it.

According to the personnel director of a large petrochemical corporation, "I had this guy come to New York from Chicago for an interview. I liked his credentials. Lots of first-rate experience and a high degree of effectiveness. When I took him to meet the department head, everything looked good. No problem with salary. An easy hire!

"Then this one detail came up. When I offered to reimburse him for his travel expenses, he told me he had driven down from Chicago. He asked for compensation for mileage and tolls. I asked for his toll receipts for the accounting people. And he got upset. He didn't have them.

"I told him to save them on the way back and mail them to me. Then he got really upset.

"It turned out he didn't drive at all. He added up the tolls and mileage rate and it came to $90 more than he had paid for the train fare. Big deal! Look what it cost him.

"Cheap shots never get you anything. They don't work around here. And neither does anyone who tries to get away with them."

Finally, just about every professional interviewer who shared stories with me had his or her own variation on this theme: "You'd be surprised how many people walk out of here without asking for the job!

"It's such an obvious mistake. An interview is like any sales call. You're selling something to me. You.

"So you need to use sound principles of salesmanship.

"First, you build a foundation of solid communication between us. You need to get into relationship with me instead of trying to impress or overwhelm me.

"Next, you need to press through my considerations and reservations about you. Get me to express them. Don't resist them or defend yourself against them and they'll all disappear.

"Finally and most importantly, at the very end, you need to enroll me in your cause. And get me to commit myself.

"The only way to do that is to stick your neck out and ask me for the job. You might even have to ask me for it twice. Or three or four times. But if you keep at me, I'll hire you!"

Asking for the job is the payoff. If you see one person, ask once. If you see two people, ask twice. If you see three people, ask three times. Asking for the job will secure the seconds you've earned in this last stage of the interview.

Never leave anyone's office without it.

---

## HOW TO GAIN SECONDS

- Have a salary in mind before you go in for the interview.
- Don't disclose it until the interview shifts in your favor.
- Let the interviewer bring up salary first.
- Work toward a salary based on your worth to the company.
- Know industry average salary levels so you can ask for more than that.
- Make sure there are no details left uncovered before you leave your interview.
- Be careful. There's still time to blow it.
- Ask for the job before you leave the interview.

# 0:50
# Following Up

As suddenly as it began, your interview is over.

It may be all wrapped up in one visit. Or it may involve two or three sequential or separate and scheduled stages with different people. Many good jobs are not often offered at the first interview.

It's all the same. Sooner or later, an end point will be reached. And you will have gone as far as you can go. For the time being.

The first thing you'll notice is one of three possible outcomes.

You walked out with the job.

You walked out without the job.

You walked out not knowing which, expecting a telephone call by a certain agreed-upon date.

What you need to do now, and I mean right now, regardless of the outcome, is to find a quiet place where you can sit down and record all of your impressions while they're fresh in your mind.

The place could be the front seat of your car, a stool in a coffee shop or even a park bench. The material to write down is the same, whether or not you got the job yet.

Start by answering the following questions in your file folder about the company where you've just had your interview.

What went right?

What went wrong?

What was discussed?

What wasn't discussed that you wish had been covered?

What did the interviewer say about you?

How did you handle yourself?

What questions surprised you or caught you unprepared?

Did you or will you get the job?

When your summary is complete, add two short lists to your file.

First, write down everything that the interviewer thinks about you after talking with you. Focus especially on job-related aspects but include personal impressions also.

Second, write down everything you now think about the company where you've just been, basing your opinions exclusively on your interview impressions.

Now you're almost finished.

But not quite.

I want you to do one more thing before your internal pictures fade. Take the time to add to your notes a rough draft of the letter that you will type up and mail as soon as you get home.

In your letter:

Thank your interviewer for the time and attention that he or she gave you.

Restate the three most positive things about you that you said during the interview.

Correct the one or two most negative points that came up by turning them into positive assets. For instance, if the problem is that you never went to graduate school in your field, but you have had three years of highly specialized, practical experience instead, now is the time to tell what's so great about that.

Close your letter with one new item of importance about your work or your background. It should be something you either forgot or didn't have time to bring up during the interview.

Sign off with one sentence that acknowledges one of the following conditions of life. (1) The job offer you got, which you'll respond to by the time you promised you would. (2) No job offer now but your expectation of being considered for another position in the future. Or (3) Notification of a job offer by the date they agreed to contact you.

If you saw two or more people, draft two or more different letters. Yes, it's a lot of work. But, "Nothing is more annoying than to route an applicant's letter to a department head and to have the same letter sent back with a duplicate attached," says the personnel manager of a corporation that leases business equipment.

Many other personnel people told me they agree. They commented that your follow-up letter earns the last few seconds you want and need to get the job in 60 seconds if you meet these criteria:

"My name and title have to be written correctly and spelled accurately."

"I don't want to get the same letter I got yesterday or five minutes ago from someone else. Every person I ever talk to is unique. That quality of uniqueness needs to come through."

"I keep a dead letter file under my desk. It's the place where I crumple up and chuck letters that lack aliveness and freshness."

"Can't stand mistakes in typing or spelling. That kind of sloppiness is certain to show up at work."

"The best letters I get are the ones that renew my interest in the applicant and cause me to take his employment here more seriously. It's some subtle motivational shift that a good letter always produces in me."

"I remember receiving two letters during my seven years here from people I turned down which were so inspiring that I actually reversed my decision, called them up and made offers. One of those people is now our national sales manager."

Listen to those people. You may very well be interviewed by one of them. Be certain that your letter covers each of their points. Draft it immediately after the interview so that it's fresh and original. And get it into the mail no later than twelve hours after that.

This next part is for you only if you do not get the offer for the job you want.

Not getting a job offer means you didn't carry out your intention. Read this checklist carefully, answer each question truthfully and you'll see exactly what went wrong.

Did you really want *that* job?

Did you set up each step of your Job Game as it is described in 0:05?

Did you tell everyone you know what your intentions about getting a job are?

Did you do the first impressions exercise in 0:10?

Did you keep your aliveness and enthusiasm in high gear?

Do you know what the best things about you are? (If not, see 0:15.)

Do you know what you don't want them to know about you? Are you sure? (If not, again see 0:15.)

Did you match your background to what they needed and wanted and did you make it fit?

Did you take the time to go to the library and do your general homework before contacting the company?

Did you follow the resume and letter writing guidelines in 0:25?

Did you do the "I Spy" homework in 0:30?

Did you do enough of it?

Did you follow the pre-interview preparation suggestions in 0:35?

Where did you hold back?

Where else did you hold back?

And where else did you hold back?

If you didn't participate at a 100 percent level, what do you expect? You can't win your Job Game unless you stick to the rules. Remember. Whose game is it? Whose rules are they?

Look at the steps you left out and make your corrections.

Then, call the interviewer who turned you down and get him to help you avoid making the same mistakes twice. Ask him to tell you the truth about where you went wrong.

See whether you can get him to be specific, even if it hurts.

Then tell him you intend to take care of all that. And ask if you can keep in touch so you can be first in line to be considered for the next opening that comes along.

You've got to do all this. No kidding. If you don't, even if you're lucky, your chances of blundering into a job are somewhere between 0.01 and 11 percent. And you don't need this book to play that small and hopeless game.

What you need to do right now, whether you decide to really use this book or not, is to examine what's going on for you about failure and rejection.

So sit down in a chair.

And think of a time when you failed or were rejected. Take the first time that comes up.

Ask yourself these questions about it.

How old were you?

Where were you?

What happened?

How did you feel?

What thoughts did you have?

What did people tell you about it?

Then think of an earlier time when you failed or were rejected. And ask yourself the same questions.

Then think of a still earlier time. Same questions.

Keep going back for as long as you feel heavy inside. After a little while, you'll reach a breakthrough point and the issue will begin to lighten up. When you begin to feel lighter about it, you've done enough for now.

And you can go right out and get a job.

This next part is for you if you're waiting to hear from them about your job offer.

Once a day, take out your folder and read quickly through your notes. Then visualize your interviewer. This time let's assume it's a man.

Close your eyes and form a mental picture of him on the back of your eyelids. See him thinking about you and deciding that you are the one. See him dialing your number and calling you up. See and hear how happy he is to be offering you your job. And let the conversation come to a close as you hear yourself tell him you'll let him know your answer within twenty-four hours.

Then close your folder and put it away, go through this process once a day for each job that you are seriously considering. The effect is to keep your intention focused on the results you want. The reason you need twenty-four hours to call back is that it will take that long to decide which job you're going to take out of all the offers you're going to get.

If your interviewer promised to call you in three or four days and doesn't, you need to call and remind him that you're alive and waiting to hear about the job. If no time to call was specified, wait one week and then call him.

Be warm and receptive, even if you have a little difficulty getting your call through.

Hang in and hang on. Don't hold back. Recap your best features and qualifications. Restate whatever promises you remember him making to you. Suggest your willingness to meet other people at the company, or to provide additional references or supporting data.

If you want to crapshoot, gently mention a competitive offer that requires your attention in the next day or two. Just don't try to hammer your way in with it.

Pressure tactics don't work. Persistence and availability do.

So be both. Persistent and available. The job you want is now just a few seconds away.

---

## HOW TO GAIN SECONDS

- Write down everything that went wrong and everything that went right. Immediately after the interview.
- Write and thank your interviewer for his or her time.
- Restate your three most positive points in the letter.
- Correct your one or two most negative points in the letter.
- Close the letter with a positive new item.
- Draft different letters for as many different people as you saw.

# 0:55
# The Final Cut

What I want you to know is that you have not yet won your Job Game. As good as everything may look, and as close as you may be to the job you want, it's not too late for it all to disappear, like mist, right before your eyes.

So if you are a person who tends to let success and happiness fly from your grasp when you are 99 percent of the way to the finish line, this is the time to examine your patterns.

Right now.

More people than you can imagine are actually much more afraid of succeeding than they are of failing.

If you're wired up that way, you can always blame your failures on someone or something else.

You're never responsible for what happens. It's always the circumstances that do it to you. And when something good happens, it's just luck. Or an accident.

The reason for this widespread fear of success is that succeeding is a true acknowledgment from the universe of how tremendously powerful you really are.

Once you open up to the idea that you can choose to have it any way you want it, and that it is well within your power to have your life work, it becomes increasingly difficult for you to blame other people or other circumstances for what happens to you. Ever again.

See how strongly you are run by your own fear of succeeding. And how it affects you. Use page 117 or take out a blank piece of paper. Do it now.

At the top, write a heading that says: The bad things about succeeding are.

Then make a list of bad things about it. Don't stop writing until you have ten or fifteen bad things about success listed. Twenty-five or thirty are even better.

What you will see emerging on your piece of paper is a pattern that you've always had. One that you can't afford to continue any longer.

The way to break up the pattern is simply to notice that you have it. And to become fully conscious about those times when you quietly fall into it.

If you don't think you get the point yet, use page 118 or turn the piece of paper over and write another heading: The good things about failing are.

Fill in a list of as many things as you can that are good about not making it. You'll be amazed at how many great things you'll think of that have been keeping you

The bad things about succeeding are:

_____

_____

_____

_____

_____

_____

_____

_____

_____

_____

_____

_____

_____

_____

_____

_____

_____

_____

_____

_____

_____

The good things about failing are:

_____

_____

_____

_____

_____

_____

_____

_____

_____

_____

_____

_____

_____

_____

_____

_____

_____

_____

_____

_____

in a pattern of failure. And that's not bad or wrong either. It's just interesting to see, finally and conclusively, how you've been stepping on your own feet and tripping yourself up.

Once you see that, it gets easy. You can simply choose not to do that anymore.

Remember back in 0:05 when you set up the rules 'or your Job Game and then examined your intention to get the perfect job for you.

Well, the perfect job for you is the one you're about 'o get.

And you need to keep re-examining your intention to get it now. Then re-examine it again twice a day until you receive the offer that nails it down for you.

Intention is a funny thing.

Keep actively in touch with it and you'll never have less than you've always wanted. In fact, what you want is what you'll get. And what you get will also turn out to be what you wanted. Every time.

But drop your intention, even for a moment, by sitting back and congratulating yourself too soon or becoming unconscious and forgetful of your goals, and as sure as the sun sets in the West, your life will turn to mush. Then you'll have to start generating new intention all over again from the bottom of the pile.

So while they're sorting out their impressions of you and your competitors, keep your intention focused on getting that job.

And while they're narrowing down the field to you and one or two other people for their final cut, keep intending for the job you deserve to come your way.

Intending is nothing like hoping or wishing or believing or positive thinking. It is knowing with certainty that you can have everything you want as long as you keep choosing to have it that way. And then choosing to have it exactly the way that it is. Moment by moment by moment.

Once you do that, you've got it made. Because you'll always know that whichever way it turns out is the way that you set it up.

That is real power. And no one else who applied for that job has a chance against you while you are exercising it.

The power of intention explains flukes and otherwise unexplainable stories that you sometimes hear.

Like these.

"The strangest experience I ever had was hiring a man who was so nervous that he wet his pants during the interview," says one of the personnel managers of a Fortune 500 company. "I guess he really wanted the job so much that I just had to give it to him."

"My most unusual hiring story is giving a job to a man who showed up for his interview wearing a dress," confided the vice president of a small computer company. "His qualifications were good. No contact with our customers was required. And, besides, he convinced me that we didn't have any of his particular minority group working here."

The personnel director of a heavy industrial machinery corporation tells this one: "I interviewed a young graduate student at a Job Fair and liked him enough to invite him to the company. He was friendly and personable. The department heads were impressed. As a formality, I checked his references. He had listed a couple of professors and other people in various industries. Each one of them turned out to be a relative!

"The guy had enough moxie to put his father-in-law, two uncles and an aunt on his reference list. Strangely enough I had a positive reaction. I thought it was cute. He got the job!"

"Here's a funny one," says the personnel director of an insurance company. "I received a resume from a fellow who was a former lineman on a pro football team. In capital letters, he listed his height as 6'3" and his weight as 225 pounds.

"When my personnel manager brought him in, he was obviously only 5'8" or so. And he looked like he weighed at least 300 pounds. I liked him anyway.

"Then he took our standard psychological tests and the results came back stamped 'Not Recommended'. I don't know why but I still liked him.

"Something about him told me that he was just fine for the job I had open. I told him all the considerations I had and made him an offer. I remember adding that if he let me down I would personally kick his butt all around the building. Later, I laughed. The guy was so powerful, he could have pulverized me with one hand before breakfast!"

Each of these people strongly intended to get the jobs they got. So they got the jobs. Either in spite of or because of their quirks.

Back to business. All this time they've been making their final selection. And you get the offer.

A happy, cheerful, congratulatory telephone call lets you know that your Job Game is over. But is it?

Not yet.

If you applied for more than one job and kept your intention high, you'll get more than one offer.

So now you get to make your own final cut. Follow these guidelines and you'll end up with the ideal choice.

Allow yourself at least a full day to run through your files on each company that offers you a job.

Compare the statistical data from your library trip. And carefully evaluate your post-interview impressions of the people, your reactions to the corporate environment, your assessment of the opportunities and growth potential there.

If you feel stuck because it seems as though you have no obvious choice, trust your intuition and your body sensations.

Tuning into your body sensations is easy. A warm satisfied feeling in your chest and solar plexus tells you that you've found your next company.

A feeling of anxiety in your stomach and intestines, tightness in your jaw and the back of your neck or a shortness of breath are all warnings that something is not right.

Learn to notice the differences between warmth, excitement and enthusiasm and anxiety, tension or deadness in your body. You'll never make a wrong choice between two alternatives again.

Notice, too, now that all the offers have been made, everything is just as it was when you designed your Job Game. Your intention is the one factor that makes a difference in the world of business, commerce and employment just as it is in every other area of your life.

Whenever it is your intention to get the job in 60 seconds, your intention will produce the job for you. In 60 seconds.

## HOW TO GAIN SECONDS

- Examine and re-examine your intention and keep in touch with it.
- Keep your intention focused on the job you want.
- Re-read all your files if you have more than one offer.
- Trust your intuition whenever you have to decide between offers.

# 0:60

# You Got It

Congratulations.

Ever since the first chapter, when you began to [illegible] the way everything really works, you have been creating the framework for holding a prospective employer's attention for a total of 60 seconds.

You did.

And you got the job.

That's great.

Now that you've got it, if you go back to your same old patterns and leave everything to chance and circumstances, perhaps with a little luck you can keep that job forever. One personnel director commented, "Except for company cutbacks, I've never seen a layoff for nonperformance. I've seen people shifted around, moved to other departments, made a little uncomfortable. But once you're on the ship when it leaves the harbor, they never throw you overboard."

Or perhaps you'll get back into the same old rut that got you out looking for another job in the first place. You'll develop a personality conflict with your boss or feel neglected or ignored or just lose your enthusiasm. And you'll start to show up for work every day feeling tense or angry or depressed. Your bright new job will slowly and surely turn into a dull old job, just like your glamorous new car always turns into a rusty old clunker.

Only none of that is really the way you want it to be. Is it?

I mean, why would you want to go to all the trouble of getting this new job if you're only going to let it turn into another old job that you have to leave in a year or two?

You don't have to do that anymore.

Now that you know how to create what you want in your life by letting your intention be bigger than circumstances or competition or any other considerations, you have an opportunity to turn this job you always wanted into a job that you will always want.

Here is how to do it.

You can't ever put your feet up and let your intention drop away. You can't ever let yourself become unconscious about what you really want to get out of your job. You can't ever turn into a victim who blames other people or events for things you don't like in your life. You can't even make anybody else wrong any more.

What you want to do instead is exactly what you've been doing to get the job.

Create your game and give it a name.

Be sure that it's your game.

Set up your rules.

Be sure that they're your rules.

Keep checking your internal experience of yourself, your body sensations, your emotional flow, your thoughts, and your first impressions and conclusions against your observations of external reality. And notice whenever something doesn't seem to fit correctly.

Do your homework and stay on top of whatever is needed and wanted on the job, so that you can volunteer new ways to take care of it.

Keep looking for more and more ways to make a contribution. And tell your boss that you are making it your job to see that he or she will always look good as well as to keep upgrading your results.

Participate. And let your participation make a difference.

Once you choose to make it all your game and to play it full out at a 100 percent level, who knows what you can accomplish and win?

Who knows?

You do.

You could get a raise in 60 days. You could get a big promotion in six months. You could even get your boss's job in 60 weeks. Or the Chairman of The Board's job in 60 months.

It all starts with the job you got in 60 seconds.

That's how it works.

And now that you've got it, enjoy it.

# Job Hunting Success:
# The Key Questions

| |
|---|
| Have I acknowledged how first impressions work? |
| What do I really want to do? |
| Where do I really want to work? |
| What company do I want to work for? |
| What position and salary do I want? |
| Does my resume express what I have to offer? |
| Did I do my homework? |
| Can my interviewer hire me? |
| Did I ask for the job? |
| Have I followed up completely? |
| Is it still my intention to get the job? |
| Can I have the job? |
| I got the job. |

# 60 Seconds Worth of Strategy for Getting a Job

:00  Get the idea that everyone makes choices based on first impressions.

·01  Begin to notice that your first impressions are as important as anyone else's.

:02  Acknowledge your ability to create and affect other people's first impression of you.

:03  See how your intention can determine the success or failure of everyday encounters.

:04  List in detail all the good things and all the bad things about working.

:05  List in detail everything you want people to know about you and everything you want to hide.

:06  Accept and acknowledge your attitudes, evaluations and judgments about yourself.

:07  Notice that there is no difference between what you think of as being good or bad about yourself.

:08  Notice that you're bigger than any items you think of as being good or bad about yourself.

:09  Choose what you want to do in life.

:10  Create a job game in which, when you win it, you get what you want to do in life.

:11  Make it your own game and write your own rules to play it by.

:12  Make your game real by telling everyone about the job you're going to get, when you'll get it and how much it will pay.

:13  Begin your game by scanning want ads and noticing your first impressions.

:14 Don't answer any of the ads you scan, even the ones you like.

:15 Don't ever answer blind ads with box numbers.

:16 Don't let employment agencies handle you on an exclusive basis.

:17 Begin to choose the companies you want to work for. Make a list of them.

:18 Start a file for each one.

:19 Go to your library and thoroughly research each company, its management and its current market strengths and weaknesses.

:20 Don't play the numbers game. You can't check out that many companies.

:21 Write your resume, presenting the relevant facts about yourself truthfully.

:22 Shorten your resume and make it neat.

:23 Make sure your name, address and phone number are at the top of your resume.

:24 Write a short letter to the person who is the ultimate authority for hiring you.

:25 Tell why the company needs and wants you and your skills.

:26 Write the letter the way you speak. Avoid unnecessarily stiff formal language.

:27 Ask for an interview, not the job.

:28 Present yourself so strongly that they will create an opening for you that fits your qualifications, even if they don't have one.

:29 Avoid long telephone conversations.

:30 Prepare for each interview by completely and thoroughly digging up all the data and all the dirt you can about each company.

:31 Use friends who work for each company for inside information.

:32 Be creative with anonymous phone calls or personal visits.

:33 Catalogue everything that's unique and advantageous about yourself and use it.

:34 List every possible question that could come up.

:35 Prepare an answer for every question and identify yourself completely with every answer.

:36 Rehearse every answer in front of a mirror until you're comfortable with it.

:37 Wear your interview clothes at least once before your interview.

:38 Look and dress as much like your interviewer as you can.

:39 Do everything you ordinarily do on the day of your interview.

:40 Bring along extra copies of your resume and any relevant material.

:41 Bring along a notebook and a pocket dictionary.

:42 Get to your interview at least ten minutes early.

:43 Monitor your impressions of the company's environment.

:44 While you're waiting, clear yourself of any confusion that might affect your impression of the interviewer and job.

:45 Notice your first impression of your interviewer and who he or she reminds you of. Then consciously let all of that go.

:46 Notice that your interviewer is having a first impression of you and seeing how closely you measure up to expectations. Don't evaluate what you notice.

:47  Answer each question quickly and succinctly.

:48  Stick with prepared answers. Do not ad-lib.

:49  Pay attention.

:50  Don't answer questions you aren't asked.

·51  Keep monitoring your aliveness and enthusiasm and keep them at a high level.

:52  Avoid salary discussions until the final stage of the interview.

:53  Ask for what you're worth. Make it more than the industry average and don't be greedy.

:54  Ask for the job before you leave.

:55  Update your file immediately after each interview.

:56  Follow up each interview with a well-thought-out letter.

:57  Keep focused on your intention to get the job until you actually get it.

:58  Be careful; it's never too late to blow it.

:59  Trust your intuitions and gut feelings when choosing between offers.

:60  Congratulate and acknowledge yourself. You got the job. Now keep your enthusiasm high and keep moving forward.

# Afterword and Acknowledgments

It's bound to come up. So let's just cover it now and get it handled.

Someone will come along, look at this book, and notice that the person who wrote it has been a self-employed writer since 1975. A normal, reasonable question will follow that observation. Like: How can a person, who has not had a job that long and does not want one, tell you how to get one?

So here's the answer. And three reasons how.

First, in my last job as Vice President and Creative Director of an advertising agency, I was responsible for hiring other creative people. I talked with lots and lots of writers and would-be writers who were looking for jobs. At least two to four a week for more than five years.

I was always aware of and fascinated by my unerring sense of knowing who would get hired next and which ones would eventually make real contributions to advertising. It usually had nothing to do with their portfolios or their resumes or their clothes. It was something else.

Today I know what that something was and why I hired who I hired. Or why someone else did or didn't. It all clicked in place instantly when Frank Molinski, my publisher, shared his first impression about a batch of job applicants that he had just interviewed and suggested the concept for this book.

Second, the kind of advertising consulting work I do now is no different from looking for a job. Except when I am consulting, I look for many jobs many times each month. Each time, I go through the same process I wrote about for you. I create my game for work each week. I target for results. I put my intention out into the universe. And I meet my targets and materialize my results. Look, I'm still doing it that way after more than seven wonderful years. And I'm not exactly starving either.

So I can tell you firsthand. The process works for getting work. The process even works for getting my books published. As I said in one of the chapters, it works for everything. Including relationships, health, money and results in every other area of life. And it will work for you. No kidding.

Third and finally. You don't even have to take my word for it. Take the word of all the people I talked to, read about and learned from, as well as the people who shared personal experiences with me that supported and confirmed my premises.

Accordingly, I want to thank each of the following for their contributions both to the content of this book and to the content of my life while I was writing it. Each of them made my Writing Game for *Get A Job in 60 Seconds* easier and more enjoyable.

Ron Abell
Herb Alexander
Ina Ames
John Barnard
Helen Beyer
Priscilla Boettcher
Nathaniel Branden, Ph.D.
Mary Ann Brody
Lorie Bruno
Amanda Burgoon
Steve Cavanagh
Richard J. Coogan
Carolyn Coulter
Paul Crimi
Budd Daniels
Joanna Daum
Paula de la Flor
Lisette M. de Miranda
C. Jo Dorr
Carol Dubin
Werner Erhard
Rosemarie Fernandez
Dick Fewkes
Dorothy Fink
Ted Fiske
G. Patrick Flanagan, Ph.D.
Harry Folger
Charles Fraggos
Rosanne Glickman
Jack Godler
Jane Graham
Jan Hulien
Ralph Indrasano
Philip Johnson

Leonard Kanzer
Stan Kaplan
Leon Kirschenbaum
John Knight
Randolph Kravette
Sanford Kravette
Murray Kremer
Shaun Levesque
George Lewis
Anna Lipworth
Julie Manga
Warren Manning
Jim McLellan
Tom Michaelson
Marilyn Miller
Frank David Molinski
Joan Mullan
Judy Meyers
Mark Meyers
Edna Nightingale
Carol Palmer
Melvin M. Ratoff
Verne Schildhauer
Karol Senecal
Jim Sinatra
Lynn Stelmah
Jerry Straus
Pascal Tchakmakian
Norma Turner
Don Ulen
John Wall
Barbara Willard
Michael Vallas
Rosian Zerner

## ABOUT THE AUTHOR

STEVE KRAVETTE is a free-lance writer who lives in Cohasset, Massachusetts, and who has authored two previous books, *Complete Relaxation* and *Complete Meditation*. He is currently a creative/copywriting consultant for a wide variety of advertising clients. He is also a stress and relaxation therapist and a musician. He is now working on three new books. He was the Vice President and Creative Director for a Boston advertising agency. In addition to his other duties, he had complete responsibility for hiring the people for his division. Since beginning work on *Get A Job in 60 Seconds*, he has been invited to be a featured speaker at a number of job and career seminars.